Los Angeles

A Pictorial Celebration

by Jon & Nancy Wilkman

Photography by Elan Penn

STERLING

New York / London
www.sterlingpublishing.com

Design by Michel Opatowski
Edited by Jennifer Sigler
Layout by Gala Pre Press Ltd.

Penn Publishing gratefully acknowledges the following institutions and individuals for allowing photographs from their collections to be reproduced in this book:

Aquarium of the Pacific 120. 121
Beverly Hills Hotel 50–51, 58
California African American Museum 154, 155
California Institute of Technology 122, 123
California Science Center 118
Catalina Island Chamber of Commerce 44, 45
Griffith Observatory 126, 127
Japanese American National Museum/Don Farber 149
Jeff Lewis/Icon SMI/Corbis 115
Joseph Sohm/Visions of America/Corbis 61, 82, 104, 113
Knott's Berry Farm 110, 111
Larry Falke courtesy of Southwestern Law School 57
Library of Congress 10, 14, 17, 19
Los Angeles Public Library 20
Los Angeles Public Library/Herald Examiner Collection 22, 23
Los Angeles Public Library/Hollywood Citizen News 21
Los Angeles Public Library/Security Pacific Collection 6, 7, 8, 12, 13, 16, 18
Los Angeles Philharmonic & Hollywood Bowl/Federico Zignani 108, 109
Los Angeles World Airports 74, 75
Museum of Latin American Art 158, 159
NASA/JPL-Caltech 124, 125
Nik Wheeler/Corbis 83
Norton Simon Art Foundation 86, 87
Petersen Automotive Museum 68
Port of Los Angeles 73
The Colburn School 90, 91
The Huntington 80, 81
The Museum of Contemporary Art/Marissa Roth 88
The Museum of Contemporary Art/Brian Forrest 89
The Paley Center for Media/Grant Mudford 101
Universal Studios Hollywood 102, 103
Wilkman Productions, Inc./Jon Wilkman 33, 56, 63, 98, 112, 137, 156

Special thanks to Roy & Chris Matalon for contributing their time, knowledge, and expertise to this book.

STERLING and the distinctive Sterling logo are registered trademarks of
Sterling Publishing Co., Inc.

Library of Congress Cataloging-in-Publication Data Available

10 9 8 7 6 5 4 3 2 1

Published by Sterling Publishing Co., Inc.
387 Park Avenue South, New York, NY 10016
© 2008 by Penn Publishing Ltd.
Distributed in Canada by Sterling Publishing
c/o Canadian Manda Group, 165 Dufferin Street
Toronto, Ontario, Canada M6K 3H6
Distributed in the United Kingdom by GMC Distribution Services
Castle Place, 166 High Street, Lewes, East Sussex, England BN7 1XU
Distributed in Australia by Capricorn Link (Australia) Pty. Ltd.
P.O. Box 704, Windsor, NSW 2756, Australia

Printed in China

Sterling ISBN-13: 978-1-4027-5036-6
ISBN-10: 1-4027-5036-6

For information about custom editions, special sales, premium and
corporate purchases, please contact Sterling Special Sales
Department at 800-805-5489 or specialsales@sterlingpublishing.com.

Opposite: View of Los Angeles from Mulholland Drive.

Contents

Understanding Los Angeles

Whether you scan the landscape from the air or explore it on the ground, one fact is undeniable: Los Angeles is *big*. The city covers more than 498 square miles. You could fit seven of America's most prominent cities within L.A.'s boundaries, with a small sliver left for the Island of Manhattan. Encompassing even more area, L.A. County is the largest in the United States, totaling 4,752 square miles. In its broadest definition, Los Angeles County contains 88 separate cities, the largest by far being the City of Los Angeles. Four million people make the city their home, and more than ten million inhabit the county. To get to know and celebrate Los Angeles may require more effort than for most cities, but the adventurous will find that L.A. rewards explorers.

Glimpses of the Past

Los Angeles is sometimes demeaned as a "city without a history." Nothing could be farther from

This picture taken in 1859 is the earliest known photograph of the Plaza. The building in its center is the city reservoir.

Santa Monica Beach, 1890.

the truth. Even so, uncovering the past in Los Angeles is challenging. A popular place to get a sense of L.A.'s most distant past is the famous La Brea Tar Pits. Here, bubbling pools of asphalt that once snared ancient mammoths and saber-toothed tigers continue to reveal a legacy of bones that paleontologists use to understand the environment 25,000 to 40,000 years ago. The results of this work are displayed at the adjacent George C. Page Museum.

Los Angeles was once an isolated outpost of the eighteenth-century Empire of New Spain. The oldest reminders of L.A.'s Spanish and Mexican days are found at Mission San Gabriel Archangel, nine miles east of downtown L.A. Here, in 1771, Franciscan fathers led by Junípero Serra established the fourth of 21 Franciscan missions strung north from San Diego to the San Francisco Bay area. Reminders of L.A.'s first Spanish community are found at L.A.'s historic

heart, El Pueblo de Los Angeles, a city historic monument located on ground that was once home to a Tongva Native American village. Here *El Pueblo de la Reyna de los Angeles* (the Town of the Queen of the Angels) was established on September 4, 1781. Some of the structures surrounding the old town plaza, near the original settlement site of the 44 colonists from Mexico, reflect not just Mexican but also French, Italian, and Chinese heritages. Evidence of the emergence of American Los Angeles, which began after California became the country's 41st state in 1850, can be seen around the plaza in such structures as the city's first firehouse.

Los Angeles was part of the Southwest land booty conquered by the United States during the Mexican War from 1846 to 1848, and it was one of the wildest Wild West towns until telegraph lines and transcontinental railroads linked it to the "civilized" East. The Autry Museum of the

First automobile in Los Angeles, built by J. Philip Erie, the driver, a resident of Los Angeles at the time. Los Angeles Mayor William H. Workman is in the rear seat, 1897.

American West is a good place to explore the fact and fiction of this frontier past. The city's isolation began to end when the first train from the East arrived via San Francisco in 1876. In the 1880s, after a second rail link was established, and thanks to enthusiastic advertisements, the population exploded from a little over 11,000 to more than 50,000.

As L.A.'s climate, growing economy, and easy-going lifestyle continued to provide a virtually irresistible lure to those seeking the promise of the American Dream, Angelenos started to realize that they were not going to be able to support continued growth if they didn't find a new and much larger water supply. The Los Angeles River proved inadequate for a city whose population had a habit of doubling every decade or so. Fortunately, they found a solution 233 miles north, in the Sierra Mountains watershed of the Owens Valley. From that point, in 1913, a man-made river was brought to the city, a gravity-fed aqueduct that was considered one of the engineering marvels of the day. The original "Cascades," the final outlet of the aqueduct, can still be seen in the northeast San Fernando Valley.

With water from the Owens Valley Aqueduct, L.A. could truly take off in the twentieth century. And it did just that. During the first decade, the earliest entrepreneurs of the new entertainment art of movies started to arrive. On account of the city's year-round suitability to filming, without much interference from rain and none from snow, and because of its proximity to a variety of locales from beaches to mountains and deserts to downtown streets, early moviemakers found Los Angeles ideal for their purposes.

By the 1920s, along with movies and tourism, the local economy was driven by a powerful confluence of agriculture (especially citrus production), an almost perennially overheated real estate market, and a bonanza of productive oil fields. The prosperity of the '20s brought another population boom, from approximately 576,000 to 1,238,000. Los Angeles soon surpassed San Francisco and became California's largest metropolis.

The 1930s had Los Angeles absorbing the impact of a worldwide economic depression along with the rest of America. But it was also during this troubled decade that a new, thriving aviation industry started adding another source of strength to Southern California's diverse and powerful economy, with significance that continues to this day.

The 1940s brought another boom to Los Angeles, as the city became a major center of America's defense industry during World War II. At their peak, Los Angeles-area defense plants were producing a new warplane or -ship literally every few minutes. Soldiers and sailors were shipped to California from all over America, and they liked what they saw here: After victory, many vets and their families decided to make Southern California their home. A half million people came to Los Angeles during the 1940s, and another half million in the decade that followed.

In the '50s, new freeways promised a high-speed, auto-based way of life, and old trolley mass transit systems were scrapped. In 1957, the arrival of the Dodgers baseball team from Brooklyn was both a literal and symbolic landmark in time. This celebrated event ended the city's sense of exotic isolation at the western end of the continent, as L.A. joined with the rest of the nation to participate in one of America's oldest and most popular pastimes.

During the 1960s, Los Angeles became determined to make its image as the "city of the future" more of a reality than ever. The creation of an impressive music and theater center on Bunker Hill, once the home of wealthy citizens who lived in grand Victorian mansions, was a sign that culture in L.A. meant more than movies. At the same time, however, devastating riots in the African American community of Watts also drew attention to unsolved social problems and big-city growing pains.

Los Angeles had always had "minority" communities, but the 1970s brought record numbers of Latin Americans, Asians, and other immigrants—a phenomenon that laid the foundations for L.A.'s future as the world's most multicultural metropolis. By 1976, L.A.'s ever-increasing population had pushed it past Chicago, into the place of America's second-largest city.

This process of growth and diversification accelerated during the '80s and '90s, as L.A. institutions continued to mature and the city's economic power gained even more international significance. The 1984 Olympic Games, considered a major modern landmark for the city, were marked by record-breaking profits and a financial surplus greater than that of any previous host city.

As the twenty-first-century begins, Los Angeles—bigger and more powerful and more complex than ever—continues to exhibit the resilience and innovation that were at the heart of the city's remarkably rapid emergence as a world capital. Problems remain, and they are formidable and far from resolved, but new ideas and a number of large-scale construction

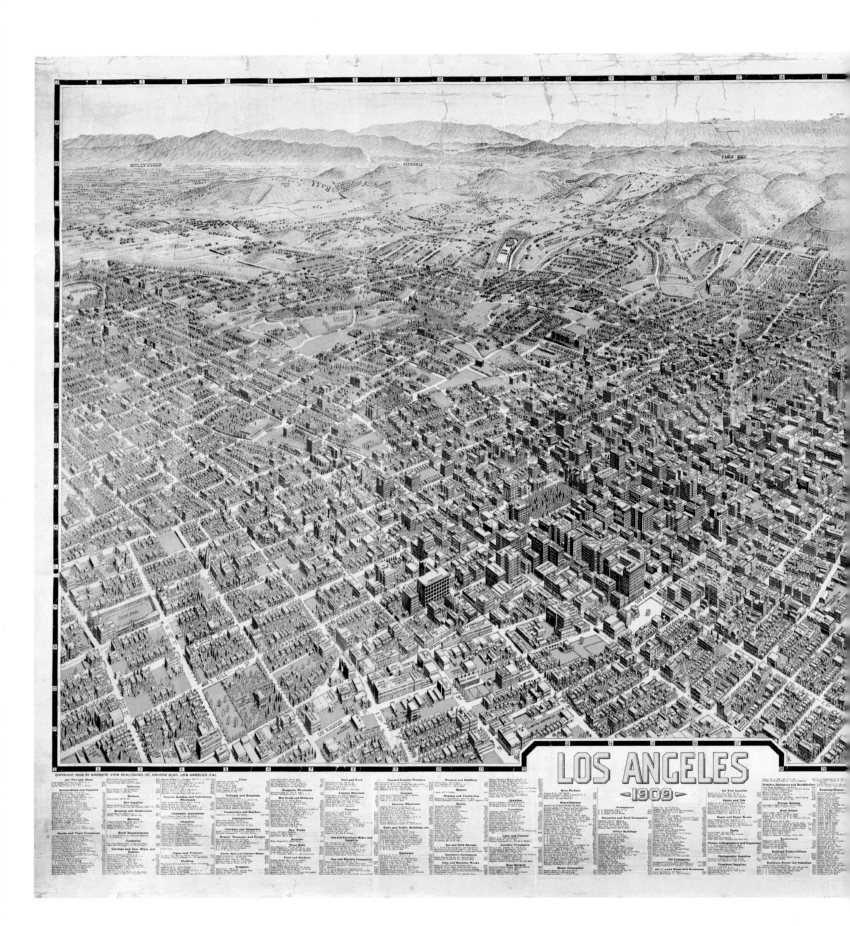

LOS ANGELES
1909

projects are also transforming the City of Angels as never before.

With Nature as a Neighbor

With the ocean on the west and mountain ranges to the north, east, and south, L.A. is often said to be set in a temperate zone, but it is actually a semi-desert environment. The average yearly temperature ranges from 56.6 to 75.6 degrees Fahrenheit, and annual rainfall averages a little over 15 inches. Today, surrounded by so much green, it's almost unbelievable that most of L.A.'s foliage consists of transplants from other places, living tributes to a nurturing climate, fertile soil, and imported water. A visit to the Los Angeles County Arboretum and Botanic Garden is a colorful celebration of this remarkable collaboration of man-made and natural environments, while a trip to the nature preserve on Santa Catalina Island will give one an idea of what the local landscape was like before man intervened.

L.A.'s natural environment bred a particular L.A. lifestyle: open and enthusiastically outdoors. For those who can afford it, living in Los Angeles provides rare proximity to natural surroundings and to every conceivable urban amenity. In the Hollywood Hills, it is not uncommon to see deer, coyotes, and even the occasional skunk living right next to homes that overlook sparkling city lights. A house in Santa Monica, a seaside community founded in 1876, offers fresh, cool ocean air and sandy beaches, as well as the famous Santa Monica Pier, with fun, carnival-like attractions.

Los Angeles is also home to America's largest urban recreational and natural preserve, named for nineteenth-century real estate magnate Griffith J. Griffith. Griffith Park offers 4,210

Los Angeles, 1909.

The Aldebaran Canal, circa 1909, later to become Market Street in Venice.

acres of wooded hiking trails, shaded lawns and picnic areas, golf courses, tennis courts, an outdoor Greek theater, and last but certainly not least, the Los Angeles Zoo. The Sepulveda Basin Parks and Recreation Area, while not as large as Griffith Park, is still definitely worth a visit, particularly as the only place from which the Los Angeles River can be seen in its natural state—

that is, bordered by willow trees and rushes instead of concrete.

Landmarks

The most famous local landmark is the Hollywood sign, originally a 1922 advertisement for a new real estate development called Hollywoodland. A more traditional monument is Los Angeles City Hall, dedicated in 1928 and the city's tallest building until the 1960s. Today, City Hall's distinctive white tower is dwarfed by a modern skyline, suggesting a diminutive mom beside overgrown offspring.

The Richard J. Riordan Central Library is one of the city's most precious architectural gems. After a devastating fire in 1993, the 1920s building was expanded and restored in a style very different from—but intriguingly compatible with—the original design. The modern addition added to the east of the original structure was built down instead of up, creating a

An overview of the celebration which took place at opening of the water runway for the Los Angeles Aqueduct in 1913. Large crowds not only lined up on each side of the runway, but also filled the field across the road (at the bottom of the picture).

THE OLD
SPANISH AND MEXICAN
RANCHOS
OF LOS ANGELES COUNTY

14

stunning five-story atrium. Architecture enthusiasts will also enjoy another 1920s landmark, the old Bullocks Wilshire department store (now home to the Southwestern Law School), an example of classic Art Deco. Newer additions to L.A.'s list of landmarks are also plentiful: The Cathedral of Our Lady of the Angels, designed by Spaniard Jose Rafael Moneo in the late '90s, is one prominent example.

As L.A. moves into the twenty first century, it's growing higher and closer together. Massive downtown edifices and development in and around transit centers are transforming the city's "autopia" heritage with pedestrian-friendly sites, both old and new. One of the old is the still-popular-as-ever Farmers Market, an outdoor complex of shops and restaurants established in the 1930s. A new one is the Farmers Market's modern neighbor, the Grove, an open-air shopping center inspired by the look and feel of a small-town Main Street, complete with an old-fashioned trolley.

A City in Motion

Los Angeles has the fifth-most active airport in the world, known as LAX, and America's busiest international harbor, the Port of Los Angeles. But when it comes to transportation, L.A. is best known as the automobile capital of the world. One recent count tallied 5.2 million automobiles registered in the County of Los Angeles. That's more than in any of 43 *states* in the U.S.! To give all these autos and their drivers somewhere to go, the city is interwoven with more than 500 miles of freeways. Visiting drivers in L.A. should always keep their eyes on the road—that is, be sure to appreciate the looping grace of major interchanges like the intertwining 110 and 105. To explore L.A.'s auto heritage at a slower—and definitely safer—pace, visit the Petersen Automotive Museum on Wilshire Boulevard, a one-stop celebration of the past, present, and future of L.A.'s love affair with cars.

Despite the fleets of automobiles and seemingly endless roadways one sees today, L.A.'s expansive urban landscape is, historically, a product of trains. During the early decades of the twentieth century, Los Angeles had the largest interurban train system in the world. But it only took until the 1950s for the individual freedom of the automobile to relegate the city's old trolleys, known as Red Cars, to the end of the line. The grand interior of Union Station and the new Gateway Center connected to it are active reminders of that golden age of train travel. In fact, as subway, light rail, and interurban trains become increasingly integral to a twenty-first-century L.A. on the move, some are beginning to wonder if they might not represent at least a partial renaissance of the city's Red Car-driven past.

The future-oriented people of Los Angeles have never had a reputation for moving backward. Many were therefore surprised when, in the 1980s, America's number one "autopia" experienced an unexpected resurgence of mass transit. In that decade, work began on both new subway and light-rail systems, and Metrolink, a heavy-rail commuter system, was inaugurated. All the projects were part of the vision of L.A.'s first African American mayor, Tom Bradley.

Art and Ideas

Because of the overwhelming influence of the movies, other forms of art and culture in L.A. often get overlooked. But that certainly does not mean that they do not exist here. One of the city's most impressive cultural landmarks is the $1 billion Getty Center, a product of the largest art endowment in history. The Getty Center complex, made up of a museum and other art and conservation institutions, is situated on a hill overlooking the Westside community of Brentwood. Another stunning product of the Getty endowment is the Getty Villa, a replicated Roman villa overlooking the beach near Malibu and housing Greek and Roman antiquities.

Los Angeles is home to a wide range of other

Los Angeles Motorcycle Club at Venice, circa 1911.

art and cultural centers, including the Los Angeles County Museum of Art, the Museum of Contemporary Art, and the Norton Simon Museum of Art in Pasadena. The city is also home to the largest collection of urban murals in the world. One of the most impressive is "The Great Wall" in the San Fernando Valley, a half-mile long visualization of California history painted on the concrete walls of a flood control channel.

Let Us Entertain You

From the 1870s, Los Angeles has been known as a tourist town. By the 1920s, it was best known as the world capital of the motion picture business. The name Hollywood is synonymous with moviemaking, but film studios are also found in Burbank, Culver City, and even downtown. Today, tourism and motion pictures have been joined at the Universal Studios Hollywood studio tour, a pre-packaged glimpse into

moviemaking that has become one of the city's most popular tourist attractions. Less elaborate but more historic tours are also offered by Warner Bros. in Burbank.

The community of Hollywood is in the midst of a major makeover, adding lavish new hotels, shopping centers, and luxury lofts alongside new restorations of classic landmarks like the Pantages and El Capitan theaters. The 1927 Grauman's Chinese Theatre, with its famous movie star foot- and handprints, is one Hollywood site that's never lost its appeal for visitors. Next door to it is a new Hollywood landmark, the Hollywood and Highland Center, a shopping and restaurant complex that is also home to the Kodak Theatre, which hosts the annual Academy Awards and many other entertainment events. Giant carved elephants loom high over the center's main courtyard, tributes to a set featured in D.W. Griffith's silent movie classic *Intolerance*.

Los Angeles is an unexpectedly active and varied theater town. In addition to major venues such as the Ahmanson Theatre and the Mark Taper Forum in the Music Center complex downtown, more than a thousand stages, small and large, are spread across L.A.'s vast urban landscape. Some of the better known include the Kirk Douglas Theater, the Geffen Playhouse, and those on the campuses of the University of California, Los Angeles and the University of Southern California. In the music scene, the Los Angeles Opera is the fastest-growing opera company in the United States, and the Los Angeles Philharmonic is acknowledged as one of the world's premier symphony orchestras.

As a longtime tourist destination, the Los Angeles area has had plenty of time to develop more than its share of appealing attractions. There's Universal Studios Hollywood and the adjacent City Walk, where visitors stroll past shops and restaurants that celebrate Los Angeles

landmarks. Nearby Orange County has the original Disneyland and Knott's Berry Farm, which claims to be America's first theme park. Disneyland still has its time-tested attractions, as well as a new "California Adventure" that attempts to encapsulate the best of the Golden State. Knott's, founded in the 1940s, has famous chicken dinners and berry pies as well as an assembly of thrill rides.

Last but far from least, Los Angeles is a major sports mecca, with championship teams to prove it. Dodger Stadium, overlooking downtown, has hosted the World Series, and Staples Center is home to the legendary Lakers basketball team. Also, albeit to the surprise of those who never associate Los Angeles with ice and snow, the city is home to the Stanley Cup-winning L.A. Kings hockey team.

A Home for Science and Technology

From advances in aviation and aerospace to sophisticated computer systems, Los Angeles has made major contributions to science and technology that have benefited not just the city itself but all America and the rest of the world. For example, after the world's first successful inter-

The set of the film, "The Squaw Man" at Lasky Feature Play Company, which later combined with the Famous Players Co., later the Paramount Famous Lasky Corporation. The first day of shooting. Cecil B. DeMille directs, December 29, 1913.

Above: Three surveyors focus on the Hollywoodland sign, erected in 1923.

Above right: Panorama along Broadway St., Los Angeles, March 11, 1946. The panorama, which looks east from North Broadway, also shows the Hall of Justice far left, and the old Hall of Records, right.

Right: Opening day of the Xth Olympiad at Los Angeles Memorial Coliseum, July 30, 1932.

national air meet was held in L.A. in 1910, L.A. aviation companies such as Douglas, Northrop, and Lockheed emerged as industry pioneers. Pasadena is home to NASA's Jet Propulsion Laboratory, managed by the nearby California Institute of Technology, one of the world's greatest educational institutions. Both the University of California at Los Angeles and the University of Southern California also have strong departments in engineering, medicine, and the sciences. While these research and technology centers are revolutionizing our lives, other L.A. science institutions tackle the task of making their work understandable—and fun—to the average person. For example, near the USC campus, the California Science Center engages and informs visitors with exhibits, hands-on interactive displays, and an IMAX theater.

Modern science and technology don't just help launch us into the future: they also provide tools to explore the past and the world around us today. A visit to Exposition Park's Natural History Museum of Los Angeles County makes that clear. Like an intriguing time machine, the museum displays the results of archaeological, historical, and anthropological studies that reveal insights into the environments and cultures of the L.A. region from its earliest Native American residents up to the twentieth century.

Two sites in L.A. offer visitors an opportunity to see further and deeper than most of them have ever seen before, and are especially fun for kids. The Griffith Observatory high in Griffith Park is dedicated to the study and presentation of outer space. The Aquarium of the Pacific in Long Beach, on the other hand, is the place for an exploration of "inner space," that is, a colorful underwater world.

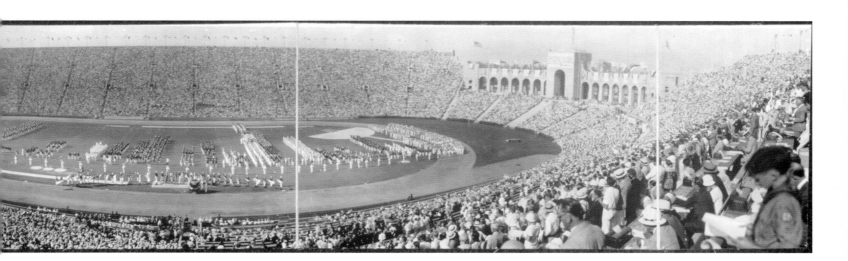

'Mr. Muscle Beach' contest at Santa Monica Beach, July 5, 1948.

At Home in L.A.

Unlike other major cities where apartments are most common, Los Angeles is best known as a city of private, single-family homes, among which are some of the finest examples of American residential architecture. Architects such as Frank Lloyd Wright, the brothers Charles and Henry Greene, and Modernists Richard Neutra and Rudolph Schindler created homes here that are today considered major works of contemporary art. Wrights' Hollyhock House in East Hollywood and the Greenes' Gamble House in Pasadena are two such architectural landmarks.

Those interested in glamour as well as architecture are usually attracted to some of L.A.'s wealthiest neighborhoods, where the homes of famous entertainment figures often live behind high walls and secure gates. These include the neighborhood around Malibu Beach, nearby Pacific Palisades and Brentwood, and older, less glamorous residential areas such as the historic West Adams District near the University of Southern California, Hancock Park south of Hollywood, and elegant San Marino east of Pasadena. Hilltop life can be found on both sides of the mountain range that spans the city: The well-known Beverly Hills, Bel-Air, and Hollywood neighborhoods are found on the southern slopes, while the San Fernando Valley side has equally impressive hideaways in the tree-filled hills of Sherman Oaks, Encino, Woodland Hills, and Calabasas.

An International Hometown

Images of fun in the sun are certainly an important part of any portrait of Los Angeles, but they're only a small portion of the full picture. L.A. is far more than simply a pleasant tourist destination. It is an economic powerhouse that ranks with entire nations, and the most multicultural metropolis on the planet. The California African American Museum and the Japanese American National Museum are inspiring places to renew one's understanding of the rich history of diversity in the United States.

L.A.'s traditional downtown can still evoke the city's past, even as it embodies the city's modern character and signals toward its future. On a typical weekend, Broadway, one of the city's major downtown thoroughfares, can seem like the *Paseo de la Reforma* in Mexico City. Thousands of Mexican Americans and recent Latino immigrants stroll past shops and restaurants there, living reminders that Los Angeles was once part of Mexico and is today home to

Bob's Big Boy on Riverside Drive in Burbank, shown here in 1954, is still a popular meeting place for teens and families.

Left: In 1957, a young fan mistakenly welcomes the Dodgers to South L.A.'s Wrigley Field. The team actually played at the Coliseum until the new Dodger Stadium opened in Elysian Park in 1962.

Right: Opening ceremonies for the 23rd Summer Olympics, the second held at L.A.'s Memorial Coliseum.

the largest Latino population in the United States. On Alamitos Avenue in Long Beach, one can get an excellent eye-full from a Latino point of view at the Museum of Latin American Art.

In the 1980s, with a population comprised of Anglos and substantial Latino, Asian, and African American "minorities," the City of Angels became the first major city in America— and perhaps the world—to not have a single "majority." There are more Mexicans here than anywhere outside Mexico. The same is true for immigrants from other Latin American countries, and for the city's Japanese, Filipino, Korean, Thai, and Vietnamese communities. L.A.'s Chinese population is second only to

New York's, and while New York and San Francisco and other U.S. cities have better-known traditional Chinatowns, Los Angeles County is home to many communities where streets lined with Chinese signs extend not just for blocks, but for miles.

The Wat Thai Buddhist temple in the San Fernando Valley, the Korean Bell of Friendship in San Pedro, and Saint Sophia Greek Orthodox Cathedral near downtown are three other sites that exemplify the breadth and depth of modern L.A.'s multicultural landscape. For the adventurous visitor or resident, exploring international L.A. can be a virtual world tour—a city definitely worth celebrating.

Glimpses of the Past

Above: Fossils recovered from the tar pits are displayed inside the George C. Page Museum.

Previous page: Heritage Square Museum.

La Brea Tar Pits

In 1769, while exploring near the future site of Los Angeles, Spanish soldiers discovered pools of a gooey substance they called *brea*, tar in English. Actually a natural asphalt, the substance had been used for thousands of years by Native Americans to waterproof oceangoing canoes, baskets, and other items. It continued to be mined freely during Spanish and Mexican rule, even after the area became part of Rancho La Brea in 1828. Access to the pits came to an end in the 1860s, when the rancho's new owner, Major Henry Hancock, began refining and marketing the asphalt.

After the Major's death, his widow leased some of the property to companies hoping to strike oil, which some did. Then, starting in 1875, diggers began turning up strange-looking bones and enormous teeth. No one gave them much attention until 1906, when U.C. paleontologist John C. Merriman learned about the fossils and, through carbon-dating, concluded that they were 25,000 to 40,000 years old. Since then, further diggings have unearthed more than three million fossils—the largest Ice Age fossil find ever. Among the specimens were the remains of ancient mastodons, bison, saber-toothed cats, dire wolves, camels, and other now-extinct creatures that wandered into the pools, got caught, and sank to their deaths.

In 1916, Major Hancock's son George gave Los Angeles County exclusive rights to excavate the pits. Seven years later, in memory of his parents, he gave the county the 35-acre Hancock Park, which encompasses the pits. Located in the Miracle Mile district of Wilshire Boulevard, the park contains a large, still-bubbling pool of asphalt and the George C. Page Museum, where visitors can see samples of the fossils and watch paleontologists at work.

Opposite: This life-size replica of an extinct mammoth seems to struggle to escape a still-bubbling pool outside the Page Museum.

Mission San Gabriel Archangel

On September 8, 1771, Mission San Gabriel Archangel became the first European institution established in the Los Angeles area. It was founded near a river that Spanish explorers named *Los Temblores* ("the tremors") after an unnerving spate of earthquakes. During rainy seasons, the river tended to overflow, and one such flood nearly destroyed the settlement. That incident led to a decision to move the mission five miles northwest to its present location in the city of San Gabriel.

With a grant of 1.5 million acres and a large number of local Indians available to willingly or unwillingly serve the mission, San Gabriel became the richest of California's 21 Franciscan missions, harvesting wheat, grapes, oranges, and olives, and boasting a herd of more than 16,000 cattle. The bustling community came to an end when California came under Mexican rule and secularization began. The cattle scattered, the fields and orchards were abandoned, and so were the Indians. Only a small diocesan church was allowed to remain until the U.S. Congress returned the chapel and immediate property to the Catholic Church in 1859.

The mission church that visitors see today is actually the third to stand on the site. Built between 1790 and 1804, it is the only one constructed of stone, brick, and mortar instead of adobe. Inside the 104-foot-long structure are the original pulpit, polychromed wooden statues carved in Spain, and a small painting of Our Lady of Sorrows. The sacristy is the best-preserved part of the structure. Behind it a museum displays photos, documents, and mission treasures, including a vestment said to have been worn by Father Junípero Serra, head of the Franciscan Order in California and founder of nine missions. The church's huge original doors are displayed outside near the *campo santo*, the final resting place of 6,000 Indians as well as the Claretian priests and brothers who have served here since 1908. The grounds also contain the ruins of the mission tannery, tallow works, kitchen, and an aqueduct, which brought water to the community.

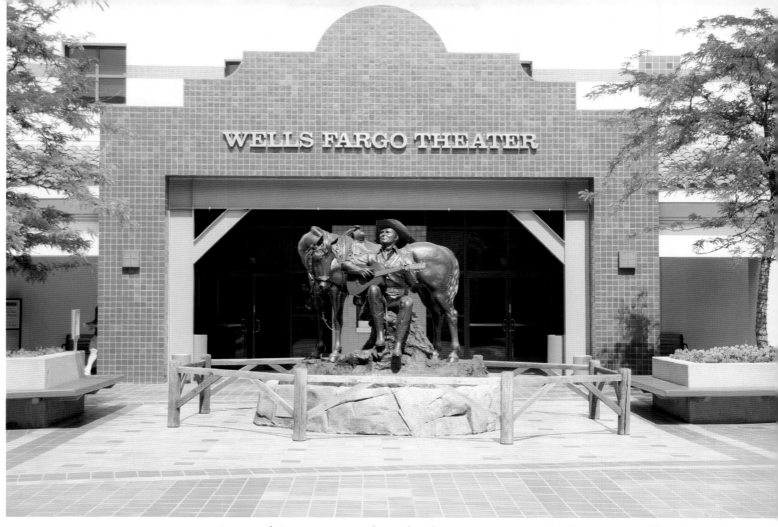

Statue of Gene Autry enshrined in bronze, a guitar on his knee, a 10-gallon hat on his head, a six-gun at his hip, and his loyal "wonder horse," Champion, at his side.

Autry National Center

Gene Autry, America's favorite singing cowboy during the 1930s and '40s, is the only entertainer with five stars on the Hollywood Walk of Fame, one each for radio, records, movies, television, and live theater. A savvy businessman as well, Autry left $320 million in assets when he died in 1998, including a chain of radio and television stations, hotels, oil wells, and the Los Angeles Angels baseball team. Ten years before his death, with major funding from Autry and his wife, the Autry Museum of Western History opened in Griffith Park with exhibits mainly exploring the mythic West portrayed in Hollywood movies and television.

In 2003, however, the museum began a process of reinvention. It merged with the Women of the West Museum and absorbed the Southwest Museum, one of the country's finest collections of American Indian arts and artifacts, founded in 1910 by the legendary author, editor, and collector Charles Lummis. It also launched the academically oriented Institute for the Study of the American West; and was renamed the Autry National Center. Along the way, the center has progressively widened its programs to include some focusing on Native Americans, African Americans, Mexicans, Asians, and other Westerners. Now, its main focus is on the intersection or "convergence" of cultures in the American West. The Autry Center is also making physical changes, adding a new wing to feature Native American objects from the Southwest Museum and renovating the original Southwest Museum structure in the Arroyo Seco to house special exhibits and educational programs.

El Pueblo de Los Angeles Historic Monument

If it hadn't been for a feisty Angelena named Christine Sterling, what remains of the birthplace of Los Angeles might have been lost forever. In 1928, the recently widowed socialite discovered that the 120-year-old Avila Adobe, the oldest home in the city, had been condemned, and the street it faced on had been reduced to a rat-infested alley. Outraged, Sterling determined to save what little remained here of early Los Angeles. "I'm only a 110-pound woman with two children to support," she said, "but I know somebody will help me." Indeed, with help from leading politicians, Olvera Street was transformed into a colorful, idealized Mexican marketplace, and seven of the adobe's original 18 rooms were restored. Now, as Sterling hoped, "every schoolboy," resident, and visitor has a place to come and learn about the city's past.

Today, Olvera Street and the Avila Adobe are among 27 designated historic structures within a 44-acre historic area. At the center, the tree-shaded Old Plaza contains a bandstand and two statues, one of King Carlos III, who authorized the Spanish colonization of California, and the other of Felipe de Neve, who chose the site for the area's first town and formally founded the pueblo on September 4, 1781. To the west of the plaza, across Main Street, is Our Lady Queen of Angels Church, or "La Placita," the oldest church in Los Angeles and the most beloved by the city's Catholic Latino community.

Directly south of the plaza stands the Pico House hotel, once the most elegant hostelry in town, built in 1870 by Pio Pico, the last Mexican governor of California. An 1884 brick firehouse, now a museum, also faces the plaza, and off a narrow cobblestone street is the Garnier Building. Built in 1890 as a community center and dormitory for Chinese workers, the building now houses the Chinese American Museum.

North of the plaza, Olvera Street is lined with shops, curio stalls, restaurants, and snack bars. Midway along the street, the restored Avila Adobe offers an opportunity to view the interior of an early nineteenth-century Mexican home. A basement museum presents a fascinating pictorial history of water in Los Angeles. Other significant structures on Olvera Street include the Pelanconi House, Italian Hall, and the Sepulveda House, further reminders of Los Angeles' early multi-ethnic and multinational history.

In 1932, the famed Mexican muralist David Alfaro Siqueiros was commissioned to paint a mural on a second-floor outer wall of Italian Hall. Titled *America Tropical*, the 80-by-18-foot work of art depicted an Indian crucified on a double cross with an American eagle above him. Although art critics initially praised the work, city leaders were outraged by its political content and the mural was whitewashed. In 1988, the Getty Conservation Institute began work to preserve as much as possible of this controversial piece of L.A. history.

Left: Shop on Olvera Street.

Bradbury Building

A jewel of late nineteenth-century Anglo Los Angeles, the Bradbury Building at 304 South Broadway reveals its charms only to those who pass beyond its exterior—described by architectural critics as "mildly Romanesque"—or who have seen its interior in one of the many films shot here, most notably the 1982 futuristic thriller *Blade Runner* and the 1950 noir classic *D.O.A.* Inside, a dark, low-ceilinged foyer leads into a central court flooded by day with light from a skylight more than five stories above. Walkways around each floor, two marble stairways, and open-cage elevators are all graced with ornate wrought-iron railings crafted in France, while the walls are faced with a pale glazed brick and the floors are of Mexican tile.

The office building was commissioned by Louis L. Bradbury, a mining millionaire turned real estate developer, and designed by George H. Wyman, an architectural assistant. The edifice would be Wyman's finest (and only major) work. During a complete restoration in the early 1990s, a new doorway was opened in the rear, connecting the building with a park honoring Bridget "Biddy" Mason, an African American slave who won her freedom after being brought to California in 1851. Biddy settled in Los Angeles, where she became a successful member of the community, eventually co-founding the local African American Episcopal Church.

The Cascades

On November 5, 1913, an estimated 40,000 Angelenos traveled by wagon, buggy, auto, and train to the northeast corner of the San Fernando Valley for the most important celebration yet in the city's history. After eight years of planning, financing, and construction, the 233-mile-long Owens Valley Aqueduct was finished, ready to deliver water to an ever-growing, ever-thirsty Los Angeles.

The idea for an aqueduct that would tap eastern Sierra Mountain snowmelt and send it to L.A. solely by gravity—with no need for pumping—came from former mayor and city engineer Fred Eaton. But it was William Mulholland, the self-educated head of the city's water bureau, who successfully oversaw the $23 million project, completing it both on time and within budget. It was also Mulholland who, after a concert, a string of speeches, and other festivities, unfurled a flag to signal the opening of the aqueduct's gates, releasing what the Los Angeles *Times* described as a "silver torrent" that "gurgled and splashed" down the concrete-stepped Cascades, a "cheerful message of good health, great wealth, long life, and plenteous prosperity to Los Angeles and her people." Mulholland famously announced to the mayor and the crowd, "There it is, take it!"

Located in the community of Sylmar, the Cascades can be seen from Foothill Boulevard and the 5 Freeway. The longer of two stepped concrete channels and the adjacent pipe carry water from the *second* Owens Valley Aqueduct, completed in 1970. The original Cascades and companion pipe, which still bring water to L.A., are halfway down the slope, on the left.

The Valley Knudsen Garden Residence dates from about 1880.

Heritage Square Museum

At the turn of the twentieth century, one of the places where wealthy Angelenos preferred to live was atop Bunker Hill in downtown L.A. By the 1930s, however, the neighborhood was in decline. In the 1960s, the hill was leveled to make room for the new Music Center and other modern structures. In 1969, when bulldozers were about to destroy two of the last Victorian-era homes, an informal group of preservationists, with the aid of the Los Angeles Cultural Heritage Board, managed to stop them. Forming the Cultural Heritage Foundation of Southern California, the group purchased a 10-acre site overlooking the Arroyo Seco that would become Heritage Square.

Over the years, members of the foundation have saved seven priceless Los Angeles-area structures by bringing them to the site and restoring them there. They include the Queen Anne-Eastlake-style Hale House; the Mount Pleasant House, whose columns and carvings suggest a wedding cake; the Mansard-style Valley Knudsen Garden Residence; the John Ford House, described as a mixture of the Italianate, East Lake, and Queen Anne styles; and a rare Octagon House, a favorite of children. Together with an 1897 church and an 1886 Southern Pacific Railroad depot, the homes form a unique museum that helps visitors to imagine Los Angeles during the period from 1865 to 1914, when the city was being transformed from a horse-and-buggy community of about 5,000 into a city of more than 400,000.

Located just off the Pasadena Freeway via Avenue 43, the museum is open most weekend afternoons and Monday holidays, but it truly comes alive on Museums of the Arroyo Day in May and on other special occasions, when costumed re-enactors serve as tour and history guides and visitors can enjoy Victorian-era food, music, and games.

Opposite: The 1887 Hale House.

With Nature As
a Neighbor

Santa Monica Pier

As early as the 1870s, Santa Monica was a favored place for visitors and Los Angeles-area residents to "bathe" in the Pacific's waters, and it still is. In addition to its wide, sandy beaches, Santa Monica is the only seaside community offering traditional carnival-style attractions as well as fun in the sun and under the stars. From 9 a.m. to midnight or later, the pier boasts a giant Ferris wheel, roller coaster, carousel, tower ride, miniature golf course, bumper cars, and traditional midway amusements, plus dramatic views of Santa Monica Bay.

The first pier on Santa Monica's beach was a privately built wooden structure erected in the 1870s. After a storm destroyed that pier, a second, 1,600-foot-long municipal pier was constructed in 1909. Then, in 1916, Charles Loof, an early amusement park entrepreneur, built his own pier next to the city's, complete with a carousel and Wurlitzer organ housed inside a fanciful hippodrome. The hippodrome has appeared in many Hollywood films and television commercials, and was named a National Historic Landmark in 1987.

As entertainment tastes changed, Loof's pier went through a series of ups and downs until, in the 1970s, it was saved from destruction by preservationists. In the 1990s, the pier was treated to a complete renovation, receiving a new concrete substructure, a restored hippodrome, and new attractions. Since its reopening in 1996, the pier has entertained millions.

Previous page: Santa Monica Beach.

Venice Boardwalk

On any weekend, in any season, the place to enjoy a little fun in the sun and free—sometimes freaky—L.A.-style entertainment is along the three-and-a-half-mile section of Ocean Front Walk known as the Venice Boardwalk. On one side of the promenade are licensed shops selling T-shirts, flip-flops, sunglasses, kites, snacks, and souvenirs, and others renting bikes, skates, and paddleboards. On the other side of the walk, unlicensed merchants display an array of wares alongside a virtual circus of musicians, jugglers, acrobats, comics, preachers, body painters, and more—all appearing in a boundless variety of dress (and *undress*), tattoos, and hair styles and colors.

Besides the usual beach for swimming and sunning, Venice Boardwalk has areas for volleyball, tennis, and basketball, a "muscle beach" section, a kiddie playground, and the

1,300-foot Venice Pier at the end of Washington Boulevard, which welcomes fishing hopefuls and even has cutouts for wheelchair-bound anglers. Another, separate paved path that runs parallel to the boardwalk is part of a 22-mile-long bikeway that stretches from Pacific Palisades in the north to Redondo Beach in the south.

Surfrider Beach

Since at least the 1920s, surfing has been synonymous with the active and playful Los Angeles lifestyle. Among the handful of beaches surfers consider the best in Los Angeles County, the very best and the most legendary is Surfrider Beach in Malibu. Stretching from the Malibu Pier to a rocky point just east of Malibu Lagoon, Surfrider is where the phrase "the perfect wave" was allegedly born.

The original inhabitants of Malibu were Chumash Indians, notable as the only Native American tribe to travel the coast in ocean-going canoes. With an economy based on fish, the Chumash undoubtedly frequented Surfrider Beach, and the remains of one of their villages is nearby. The tribe was nearly extinguished during Spanish and Mexican rule, and in 1805, a 13,316-acre portion of their land was granted to

a Spanish explorer as Rancho Malibu Sequit. The rancho was purchased in 1892 by wealthy businessman Frederick Rindge and his wife, May, to serve as their private getaway. In 1904, the couple managed to prevent the Southern Pacific Railroad from extending a line across their property. May continued to fight for privacy after Frederick's death in 1905, but eventually lost a long battle with the state, resulting in the 1926 opening of the road now known as Pacific Coast Highway, or PCH.

With the opening of the coast road, surfboarders soon discovered the one area beach that consistently produced long, smooth waves. At the same time, Hollywood celebrities, including Barbara Stanwyck, Clara Bow, and Gloria Swanson, began building beach homes along another stretch of the Malibu shore. During the

1950s, L.A. teenager Kathy Kohner began hanging out with a group of Surfrider Beach regulars, who taught her how to ride the waves—and nicknamed her "Gidget." Kohner's father, a Hollywood scriptwriter, turned Kathy's tales of her Surfrider Beach adventures into a best-selling novel, then sold the rights to a major studio. In 1959, the first of six "Gidget" features debuted, followed by a string of "Beach Party" movies and a "Gidget" television series.

Santa Catalina Island

L.A.'s only island getaway—"26 miles across the sea," according to a 1950s pop song—Santa Catalina has been a popular destination for yachtsmen, vacationers, and SCUBA divers since the 1890s. In that decade, the sons of Phineas Banning, an early Port of Los Angeles founder, developed the island's first resort and glass-bottom boats. William Wrigley, Jr., the Chicago chewing gum magnate and owner of the Cubs baseball team, purchased the island in 1919, developed the town of Avalon there, and erected the island's landmark Art Deco Casino, a ballroom that opened in 1929 and hosted big-bands and Hollywood celebrities throughout the

1930s. Wrigley also built a mansion (now a bed and breakfast) overlooking Avalon's crescent harbor, and funded the construction of the "great white steamer" *S.S. Catalina*. Together with her sister ship the *S.S. Avalon*, the *Catalina* carried visitors back and forth from San Pedro Bay until the 1970s.

Although Wrigley encouraged visitors, he

Avalon Bay.

wanted the majority of the island to be preserved in its natural state. To continue his stewardship and protect the island's native ecosystem, Wrigley's heirs created the Catalina Island Conservancy in the early 1970s. The non-profit now owns and manages approximately 88 percent of the 21-mile-long island. Travel on the island is limited to rented golf carts, but the conservancy has laid out hiking trails for those who wish to explore on foot.

In 2007, a wildfire raced through 4,200 of the island's nearly 50,000 acres. Fortunately Avalon, the only town on the island, was untouched. Its simple, laid-back charms still beckon day-trippers and vacationers to what that 1950s pop song called "the isle of romance."

Griffith Park

With more than 4,210 acres of natural *and* improved grounds, Griffith Park is the largest municipal park in the United States. Located at the eastern end of the Santa Monica Mountains, the park contains the Los Angeles Zoo, Griffith Observatory, the Autry National Center, the Travel Town Transportation Museum, and the Greek Theater. Add to that four public golf courses, many miles of hiking and bridle trails, tennis courts, playgrounds, train and pony rides, a streamside retreat in Fern Dell, and expanses of well-tended lawns, and the result is "a place of recreation and rest for the masses, a resort for the rank and file, for the plain people."

That was how businessman Griffith J. Griffith described his vision for the site in 1896, when he donated 3,015 acres of the Rancho Los Feliz to the city of Los Angeles for a public park. Griffith

was a Welsh immigrant who made a fortune speculating in California gold mines. With part of that fortune, he purchased a portion of the rancho originally granted by Spain to Jose Vicente Feliz, one of the soldiers who accompanied the founders of Los Angeles to their new home. Whether his gift was inspired by generosity or an attempt to escape heavy taxes on then-essentially undevelopable land (or both), Griffith did have a grand vision for the park—which included the Greek theater and observatory one sees there today—and he left a sizable trust to help make those dreams realities. Despite a wildfire that burned 800 acres of native chaparral and immigrant eucalyptus and pine trees in 2007, all grassy areas and major attractions are open and being enjoyed as Griffith hoped.

Sepulveda Basin Parks and Recreation Area

The six-square-mile flood-control area known as Sepulveda Basin offers residents and visitors a wealth of recreational opportunities and a unique view onto L.A.'s natural past. Located in the southwest San Fernando Valley, this is the only place where the Los Angeles River can be seen in its natural state, bordered by willow trees and rushes instead of concrete. The most convenient viewing spot is from Balboa Boulevard, where the river is identified—as it is elsewhere—by a blue sign with a white heron and the words "Los Angeles River."

The west half of the recreation area contains two public golf courses and the 27-acre man-made Lake Balboa. A popular place for families, the lake has separate sections for fishing, paddle-boating, and remote-control boating, as well as adjacent picnic and playground facilities. Part of the lake is ringed with Japanese cherry trees, which put on a spectacular display each spring. The northeast corner of the area contains a water reclamation plant and a lovely Japanese Garden. Directly south are improved parklands with picnic tables, a baseball diamond, cricket fields and, most prized of all, the Sepulveda Basin Wildlife Reserve. Developed over more than 20 years, the reserve offers the best image of what this part of the San Fernando Valley might have looked like before Spanish, Mexican, and American immigrants arrived and developed the land. From nearby parking lots, trails lead through native willows, cottonwoods, and sycamores, where goldfinches, woodpeckers, and other birds can be found. Also along the trails are lookouts over two lakes, home to migratory waterfowl as well as year-round resident mallards, American coots, double-crested cormorants, and the like.

Lake Balboa.

Los Angeles County Arboretum and Botanic Garden

The Arboretum, as the Los Angeles County Arboretum and Botanic Garden is more commonly known, is a 127-acre site with spacious lawns, tree-lined paths, and close-up views of the nearby San Gabriel Mountains. The property was once part of Mission San Gabriel's vast holdings, then part of Rancho Santa Anita, owned by Scotch immigrant Hugo Reid. In 1873, the rancho was purchased by Elias Jackson Baldwin, whose fortune (and nickname "Lucky") was gained from speculating in silver stocks. Baldwin founded on the property both the town of Arcadia and the first thoroughbred racetrack, where Santa Anita Park is today. He also built a lavish Queen Anne-style cottage on the rancho; his intention was to live there with his fourth wife, but she left the notorious philanderer before the home was finished.

After Baldwin's death in 1909, the property remained in private hands until 1947, when the State of California and Los Angeles County purchased 111 acres for a botanical garden and arboretum. Today, the Arboretum encompasses several specialized areas. The former jungle area, now a tropical forest, is where dozens of "Tarzan" movies were filmed, as well many others. The grounds also have a historic section featuring the kind of brush huts that sheltered the area's original Tongva Indian residents, a reconstructed adobe such as Hugo Reid and his Indian wife would have used, and a relocated Southern Pacific Railroad depot. Baldwin's Queen Anne Cottage and Coach Barn are nearby. Fans of 1970s American television may recognize some of these sites from the "Fantasy Island" television series.

Queen Anne Cottage designed by Albert A. Bennett for entertaining. The cottage was constructed by Elias Jackson "Lucky" Baldwin in 1881 and restored and dedicated May 18,1954 as part of Los Angeles State and County Arboretum.

Landmarks

Los Angeles City Hall

From its completion in 1928 until the 1960s, City Hall was the tallest building in Los Angeles—*by law*. At a height of 28 stories (450 feet), the structure far exceeded the city's legal limit of 12 stories (150 feet), which had been established shortly after the 1906 San Francisco earthquake. Today, even though it is now dwarfed by more than a handful of much taller towers, City Hall remains one of L.A.'s most recognizable and emblematic architectural symbols.

The building is actually the third to serve as City Hall since L.A.'s founding. To design it, the city commissioned three highly regarded local firms, headed by John Parkinson, Albert C. Martin, and John C. Austin. Martin created the structural design; Austin the working drawings; and Parkinson was responsible for the style of the building, which has been described as an "artful blend of Classical and Mediterranean traditions, with a decidedly Moderne spirit," and with beautiful interior spaces dominated by Romanesque influences. The building's lower portion was constructed of light-gray California granite, but to save costs, terra cotta was chosen as the covering for the upper floors and tower.

Some of those terra cotta portions were the first to fall during the destructive 1994 Northridge earthquake. Fortunately, no one in the building was seriously hurt during the 5 a.m. quake, but the damage raised serious concerns for the structure's integrity. The result was a $300 million retrofit that included placing the entire building on a shock absorber foundation that designers say will withstand an 8-point quake. The 27th-floor observation deck was also restored and reopened to the public, and the 1929 Lindbergh Beacon, installed to honor the airman's solo transatlantic flight, was restored and replaced atop the tower where, on special nights, it sweeps its light across the city.

Previous: The Beverly Hills Hotel.

Cathedral of Our Lady of the Angels

In 1996, 120 years after completion of St. Vibiana's, the first Roman Catholic cathedral in Los Angeles, the archdiocese decided it was time to build a new one. The 1994 Northridge quake had rendered the historic structure unsafe, and church leaders felt that Los Angeles deserved a new cathedral anyway, one more befitting of the Archdiocese of Los Angeles' status as the most populous in the country. In 2002, Cardinal Roger M. Mahoney officially dedicated the Cathedral of our Lady of the Angels. Three years later, the restored St. Vibiana's reopened as a cultural center.

Designed by Pritzker Prize-winning Spanish architect Jose Rafael Moneo and built at a cost of nearly $190 million, the new cathedral complex occupies an entire city block between Grand Avenue, the 101 Freeway, and Hill and Temple streets. While the church is an imposing land-mark when viewed from the northbound lanes of the freeway (most beautiful at night), at street level it can appear rather forbidding. Once inside the walls, however, it's clear that the complex was designed to look inward, to inspire serenity and reflection.

Visitors enter below a golden-haloed statue of the "Lady of the Angels" and through a double set of bronze doors sculpted by Robert Graham, a Mexican-born L.A. artist. A gently rising and narrowing hallway (ambulatory) ends at an ornate seventeenth-century retablo imported from Spain. A sharp turn right and a few steps later, the 12-story-high, 3,000-seat sanctuary is revealed. The sanctuary floor slopes down and narrows to focus on the altar and a monumental cross-shaped window above it. Lining the lower side walls are huge tapestries designed by artist John Nava, with lifelike portraits of saints as well as ordinary people, such as one young boy wearing shorts and tennis shoes with a lace untied. Twelve bronze dedication-candle holders designed and fabricated by Max DeMoss line the nave. A full-body baptismal font, an interfaith garden, and a long glass wall etched with images of angels are among the many other beautiful features that await congregants and visitors to the cathedral.

Richard J. Riordan Central Library

The Los Angeles Central Library, built in 1926 and renamed in 2001 to honor a recent mayor, is one of L.A.'s most beloved institutions. That fact became undeniably clear when, after a devastating 1986 arson fire, 1,700 volunteers arrived at the library to help clean up and save as many volumes as possible. Only two years before, the building had been saved from possible destruction when the city agreed to sell the building's air rights and sign a sell–lease back deal with a local developer. The $141 million arrangement covered both the renovation and expansion of the library, and allowed the developer to construct the 70-story office tower across the street. Thanks to additional donations, the library reopened in 1993 with a new, eight-story-deep wing named for former mayor Tom Bradley that features three huge chandeliers, a new garden outside the west entrance, and much-needed underground parking.

In designing the original structure, Bertram Grosvenor Goodhue drew on Egyptian, Roman, Byzantine, and Islamic traditions. His initial plans called for a domed tower top, but he changed them to incorporate the more distinctive, colorful tiled pyramid one sees today. Visitors should not miss the Lodwick M. Cook Rotunda, with its fabulous bronze and glass globe chandelier and huge wall paintings depicting the eras leading up to the founding of Los Angeles. One could easily spend an hour or more at the library studying just the building's art and architecture. But for most Angelenos, the real attractions are the millions of books, periodicals, documents, and other resources, which form the third-largest collection in the nation.

Fireworks over the Los Angeles Memorial Coliseum celebrate Fourth of July.

Los Angeles Memorial Coliseum

Designed by local architects John and Donald Parkinson, the Los Angeles Memorial Coliseum is both a state and National Historic Landmark. Since its opening in 1923, the building has enjoyed a rich and distinguished history. It hosted the 1932 and 1984 Summer Olympic Games as well as two NFL Super Bowls. It's been home field for the USC football team since it opened, and served the same purpose for USC's cross-town rival team from UCLA for half a century, from 1931 to 1981. The former Brooklyn Dodgers played home games here for four seasons until Dodger Stadium was completed in 1962, and the Coliseum even hosted a World Series in 1959, when the Dodgers won the pennant over the Chicago White Sox. Two pro football teams also briefly made their homes here: the Rams from 1946 to 1979, and the Raiders from 1982 to 1994.

In addition to athletic events, the Coliseum has welcomed its share of important public figures. Most notably, John F. Kennedy came here to accept his party's nomination for president in 1960, and John Paul II performed a Papal Mass in the stadium in 1987. The Coliseum's all-time attendance record was set in 1963 when evangelist Billy Graham drew a crowd of 134,254—more than 28,000 over the normal 106,000 limit. The Coliseum was also packed for a 1976 Bicentennial Spectacular.

Hollywood Sign

Somehow it seems appropriate that the most famous landmark in Los Angeles began as a real estate ad. The sign went up in 1923, during a decade in which the city would double its population, just as it had every decade since the 1880s. The sign originally consisted of thirteen 50-foot-tall letters intended to lure homebuyers to HOLLYWOODLAND, a new development in the hills above Hollywood financed by a group of investors that included Harry Chandler, the powerful publisher of the Los Angeles *Times*. The sales pitch continued even at night, when the letters were illuminated by 4,000 light bulbs.

With time, the sign outlived its purpose, and after a disillusioned young actress jumped to her death from atop the letter "H" in 1932, many called to have the sign removed. In 1949, strong winds finally brought down the "H," stirring embarrassed members of the Hollywood Chamber of Commerce to repair the HOLLY-WOOD part and remove the rest. But by the 1960s, the sign was once again falling apart.

In 1978 the Chamber finally came up with a viable plan. It would replace the sign with a new one that would be financed by "selling" individual letters to interested Angelenos. In the end, nine donors—including Playboy's Hugh Hefner, cowboy star and businessman Gene Autry, pop singer Andy Williams, and rock star Alice Cooper—put up some $28,000 apiece. Since its unveiling in November 1978, on the 75th anniversary of the founding of Hollywood, the sign has been a world-renowned landmark and a beacon to all those aspiring stars who come here to try their luck for fame and fortune.

The Louis XVI Room, designed by Eleanor LeMaire.

Bullocks Wilshire Building

In the half-century before the appearance of suburban malls and designer boutiques, Bullocks Wilshire was *the* department store of choice for elite Los Angeles shoppers. Located at the corner of Wilshire and Westmoreland, this branch of the once-popular department store opened in September 1929. Designed by John and Donald Parkinson, the five-story, stepped-back terra cotta and copper structure with 241-foot signature tower is recognized as an extraordinary example of late 1920s Art Deco architecture, both inside and out.

The store's location in what was then the western outreaches of the city was very strategic: right on the broad boulevard that would soon be paved 20 miles to the sea. By that time Angelenos were already wedded to the automobile, and Bullocks Wilshire accommodated customers arriving by car by having its main entrance in the rear, next to a parking lot.

When it opened, to call Bullocks Wilshire a "store" was almost unthinkable. "It's a temple," declared a Los Angeles *Times* reporter, "a temple to a courageous faith in the growth of the city" and "a temple to women." Indeed, the building housed much more than just wares for sale. There was a "relaxation room" and a "little smoking room" for female shoppers, as well as an elegant tea lounge and lunch room. Sumptuous interiors, which included murals and bas-reliefs, were designed not just as backgrounds for the stock, but to reflect the high quality of the merchandise and to create a beautiful environment for shoppers.

Despite this, in the years after World War II, development continued to move farther west and north, and business at Bullocks began to fall. The chain passed through the hands of several owners until, in 1993, the Wilshire branch closed its doors. Two years later, in a remarkable example of sensible and sensitive reuse, the building became home to Southwestern Law School. It can now be visited on special tours by arrangement with the school.

Beverly Hills Hotel

In 1912, when the Beverly Hills Hotel opened on Sunset Boulevard, only a few scattered homes dotted the area, and the city of Beverly Hills did not yet exist. But it was the hotel's express intention to lure producers, directors, and stars of the budding film industry away from Hollywood to a new, more upscale development in the area. In 1920, when Douglas Fairbanks and Mary Pickford settled into their Pickfair mansion atop a nearby knoll, the hotel appeared to have achieved its goal, as both it and Beverly Hills began playing host to the rich and famous.

Except for a low point in the early 1930s and a two-year period in the 1990s when the doors closed for a $100 million restoration, the hotel has welcomed a continuous stream of movie stars, foreign dignitaries, and less famous but still wealthy guests. Marlene Dietrich was one of several stars who lived at the hotel for extended periods, and Howard Hughes spent nearly 30 years, off and on, in a secluded suite of bungalows here.

It was during the hotel's heyday in the 1940s that the building got its distinctive pink and green decor and a new wing designed by local African American architect Paul Williams. Also during the '40s, the hotel's El Jardin Restaurant was renamed the Polo Lounge to honor Will Rogers, Darryl Zanuck, Spencer Tracy, and champion polo player Tommy Hitchcock, who used to play the game in a neighboring bean field. With this star-studded history, it's no wonder that, even after nearly 100 years, the hotel remains a favored hostelry and enduring Los Angeles landmark.

Farmers Market

In a city known for showing little regard for the past, the Farmers Market is an old-fashioned anomaly. The single-story, semi-open-air, wooden maze of fruit and vegetable stands, butchers, bakers, ice cream makers, food stalls, and curio shops is essentially the same as it has been since the late 1930s.

It's often said that the market began in 1934 as an impromptu affair, when local farmers began gathering on a dusty lot at Third Street and Fairfax Avenue to sell affordable produce to Depression-struck Angelenos. In fact, the market was one of many successful ventures begun by A. F. Gilmore, a dairyman who turned into an oil and gas distributor after he struck oil while digging for water. Before the Farmers Market, Gilmore had already built an auto racetrack on the same large block, known then as "Gilmore's Island," and he would later add a baseball stadium, home of the minor league Hollywood Stars, on the same property.

Gilmore's other structures are long gone, but the Farmers Market remains a lively and unpretentious gathering spot, enjoyed by residents and tourists alike. To the relief of the market's many fans, the upscale Grove, which opened next door in 2002, has only made the Farmers Market more popular—and more appreciated as a unique reminder of L.A.'s past.

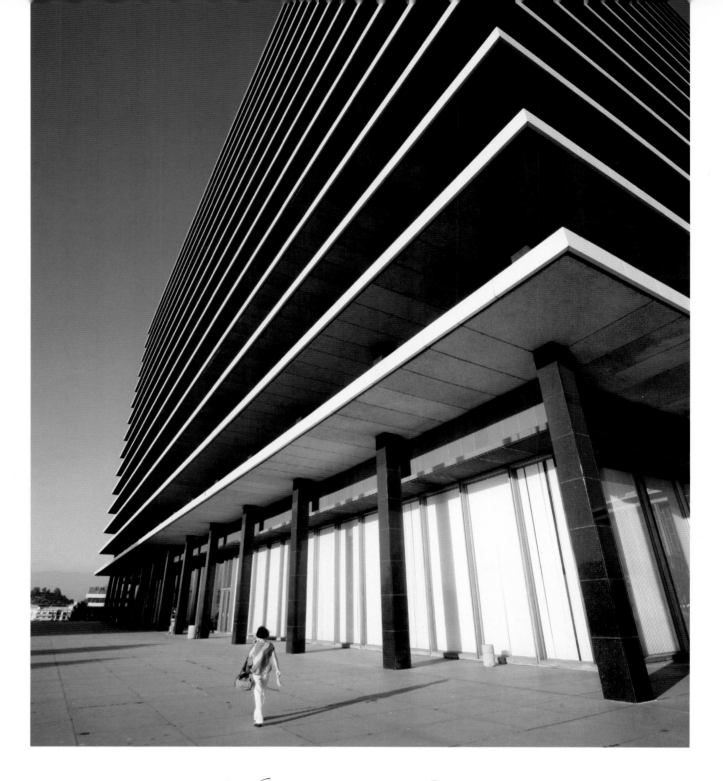

Department of Water and Power Headquarters Building

Situated at the west end of the Civic Center Mall, facing the Music Center courtyard, the headquarters of the Los Angeles Department of Water and Power was considered the most important architectural work in modern Los Angeles from its opening in 1965 until Walt Disney Hall was completed in 2003. The building was designed by Albert C. Martin and Associates for the nation's largest municipal utility. By day, the 17-story, concrete-planed and glass-sided building seems to rest ever so lightly on a thin, watery moat and an open-air parking lot below. By night, the structure is transformed into "a magnificent giant lighting fixture," in the words of one architectural critic. When amber and blue lights play on fountains that splash up out of surrounding pools at night, the effect can be magical.

Rose Bowl

This sports venue is known worldwide as the host of the annual New Year's Day college football classic following the Rose Parade in Pasadena. It was commissioned by the Tournament of Roses Association in 1921 and designed by Myron Hunt, a local architect who also designed the Henry E. Huntington mansion and literally hundreds of other homes and structures.

Set on a wide, flat section of the Arroyo Seco, with the San Gabriel Mountains as a majestic backdrop, the original 1922 Rose Bowl stadium was shaped like a horseshoe and could seat 57,000. Over the years, the arena has been rounded into the shape of a bowl and remodeled several times, so that it now seats over 90,000. The Bowl has been the home field for UCLA football since 1982, and has hosted numerous athletic and entertainment events, including five National Football League Super Bowl games, the 1984 Olympic soccer matches, the 1994 Men's World Cup, and the 1999 Women's World Cup. It was designated a National Historic Landmark in 1987.

The annual Rose Bowl classic, January 1, 1991.

Pacific Design Center

In 1975, when the Pacific Design Center opened the Blue Building at the corner of San Vicente Boulevard and Melrose Avenue in what is now part of the city of West Hollywood, it immediately became a favorite of Angelenos. With its deep-blue opaque glass exterior and a design combining flat planes with undulating forms, it was unlike any structure in Southern California and was soon given a nickname: the Blue Whale. Thirteen years later, a rich emerald Green Building was added, followed in 2008 by the Red Building, both also made of richly colored opaque glass. Each member of the trio was designed by the renowned Argentina-born architect Cesar Pelli. The Red and Green buildings are dedicated to offices, but the Blue Building contains 130 showrooms that make up the largest source of fine home furnishings on the West Coast. Sales are open only "to the trade," but visitors can window-shop and enjoy the building's other public spaces, which include a lovely central garden and a branch of the Museum of Contemporary Art (MOCA).

Hollywood and Highland Center

After decades of decline along fabled Hollywood Boulevard, the November 2001 opening of the complex of shops, restaurants, and theaters known as the Hollywood and Highland Center heralded the beginning of Hollywood's long-awaited rebirth. True, not all architectural critics were impressed, but locals welcomed the addition as a safe and fun place to eat and shop, and tourists were happy to finally have something to see and do besides muse over sidewalk stars in the Hollywood Walk of Fame and celebrity hand- and footprints at Grauman's Chinese Theatre.

Hollywood and Highland Center is located next to the historic Chinese Theatre, on the corner where the Hollywood Hotel once served as temporary residence and perpetual party place for Rudolf Valentino, Paola Negri, Gloria Swanson, and other early movie stars. The center's interior court recalls the Babylonian set for D. W. Griffith's 1916 film *Intolerance*, with a massive façade and two huge columns topped by seated elephants. Beyond the court is a platform with a tongue-in-cheek concrete "casting couch," a perfect spot to take snapshots with the Hollywood sign in the background. Inside the complex is the 3,500-seat Kodak Theatre, now home of the annual Academy Awards, and behind the theater is the revamped high-rise Renaissance Hollywood Hotel, many of whose rooms offer impressive views of the city.

The Grove

While Larchmont Village and other small community gathering places grew up naturally to meet the needs of local neighborhoods, the collection of shops, restaurants, and theaters known as the Grove is the result of very careful calculation. Located immediately east of the historic Farmers Market, the Grove was designed by a native Angeleno, Rick Caruso, to represent an idealized old-fashioned, pedestrian-friendly street. Instead of cars, the Grove's main street has a double-decker trolley (whose purpose is more entertainment than transportation). With cobblestone streets, a park-like expanse of grass, a fountain that spouts and dances to recorded music, statues of children at play, middle- to up-scale shops, and great people-watching, the Grove is an enjoyable mixture of old and new, of "free" and "for sale." That's a blend that has been wildly popular here, and is becoming a new model for shopping and entertainment centers in Los Angles and across the country.

A City in Motion

Petersen Automotive Museum

Like Los Angeles itself, Robert E. Petersen had a lifelong love affair with the automobile. The son of a Danish immigrant mechanic, Petersen arrived in L.A. in the mid-1940s as a high-school graduate with well-honed mechanical skills and a passion for cars—particularly hot rods. He helped stage the city's first hot-rod show in 1948, and to publicize the event, he launched *Hot Rod Magazine*, the first publication of what would become the largest special-interest publishing company in the country. Much later, with his wife Maggie, Petersen donated $30 million to create the Petersen Automotive Museum, which opened its doors in 1994 at the corner of Wilshire Boulevard and Fairfax Avenue, across the street from the Los Angeles County Museum of Art (LACMA).

As one would expect, the Petersen Museum displays classic autos and motorcycles. But what distinguishes the museum most is that it provides context, exploring the relationship between cars and culture and the effects each has had on the other. In the museum's permanent first-floor exhibit, titled "Streetscape: The Car and City in Southern California," visitors are led through 90 years of automotive history, brought to life in 30 exhibits, including a 1901 blacksmith shop where one of the city's first cars was built, a 1920s service station, a customizing shop, and a 1960s suburban garage. The museum's second floor is dedicated to changing exhibits that explore other, more specific themes, such as convertibles, alternative-fuel vehicles, and Hollywood movie and celebrity cars. The 35,000-square-foot building also includes an interactive discovery center for children on the third floor, and space on the fourth floor for special events.

Previous page: U.S. 101, looking north in Cahuenga Pass.

L.A. Freeways

It's impossible to *imagine* Los Angeles, let alone get around the metropolis, without freeways. The city's first freeway, an 8.2-mile stretch connecting downtown with Pasadena, opened on New Year's Eve 1939. The roadway was originally named the Arroyo Seco Parkway after the dry streambed it followed, but later renamed the Pasadena Freeway and given the state route number 110.

Today, more than 20 freeways crisscross the greater Los Angeles area with many hundreds of miles of concrete and asphalt. According to the California Department of Transportation (Caltrans), the agency responsible for the state's highways, the busiest interchange is where the 405 (San Diego) crosses the 101 (Ventura) at the northern end of Sepulveda Pass. A close second is the 10–110 (Santa Monica–Harbor) interchange near the convention center. The Marina Freeway (State Route 90) is the city's shortest freeway at about 2.25 miles in length. One of the most esthetically pleasing examples of freeway design is the 110–105 interchange: whether looking down from the air or up from the 110, there's something enchanting about the concrete swirls of the 105. The most photographed section of L.A. freeway, however, remains the four-level 101–110 interchange, dubbed the "mixmaster" when it opened downtown in 1954.

105 Freeway transition ramps above the 110.

Union Station and Gateway Center

The last great railroad depot to be built in America, L.A.'s Union Station opened at 800 North Alameda Street in May 1939, just in time to serve the thousands of servicemen who would pass through Los Angeles during and after World War II. Designed under the direction of John and Donald Parkinson in a blend of Spanish and Streamline Moderne styles, the station has 52-foot-high ceilings, marble floors, a 135-foot clock tower and—unique to stations of that era—outdoor gardens where waiting passengers can still enjoy the California sun.

As car and airplane travel became more popular after the war, the number of trains at Union Station dropped from 60 a day to only seven, and the station fell into a long period of decline. Then, in response to the needs of a burgeoning metropolitan population, Union Station was reborn in the 1990s. Within a few years, it became the hub for Metrolink's new heavy-rail commuter trains bringing workers in from Ventura, Orange, San Diego, and San Bernardino counties, and for new light-rail and subway lines operated by the Los Angeles County Metropolitan Transit Authority (also known simply as Metro). City bus connections were added in 1995 when the Gateway Center and Patsaouras Transit Plaza opened at the east end of Union Station's concourse. Here, as at every subway and light-rail station in the city, travelers enjoy original artworks, such as Richard Wyatt's 79-by-22-foot mural "City of Dreams" depicting the city's rich ethnic history. Construction of a new, 27-story head-quarters building for the transit authority, and another nearby for the Metropolitan Water District, has attracted other new developments, heralding yet another possible form of "in-fill" as the city continues to grow more upward than outward.

Opposite: Gateway Center.

Hollywood and Vine Metro Station

In the 1990s, the Los Angeles County Metropolitan Transit Authority began instituting a new policy to include art at Metro stations. The first ground-up application of the policy was on the Red Line subway route. For the initial four stations, the agency chose four different artists to create decorative artworks to enliven the stations. For each subsequent station, Metro chose an architect to design the station as well as an artist. When the first four stations opened in 1992, swarms of Angelenos jammed the cars and stations to gaze at the brilliant murals, odd sculptural flying figures, floating neon bars, and even a fanciful chandelier.

Of the fifteen stations completed, the one designed by architect Adolfo Miralles and decorated by artist Gilbert "Magu" Lujan is especially appropriate to its location at Hollywood and Vine and particularly entertaining. Walls along the entrance are adorned with fanciful tiles hand-painted with images recalling the fun of cruising Hollywood Boulevard in the 1940s and '50s. Below them, floor tiles in the pattern of a yellow-brick road, a subtle reference to the 1939 classic *The Wizard of* Oz, lead to ticket machines and, just beyond, to two antique film projectors. The station also features a movie screen with curtains drawn for a show to begin, benches with thin, stylized cars for backrests, and a ceiling completely covered with 35-mm film reels. In another whimsical touch, the handrail along one set of steps leading down to the platform is decorated with musical notes, soundlessly singing "Hooray for Hollywood."

Port of Los Angeles

San Pedro Bay was just a mire of mudflats when Spanish explorer Juan Rodriguez Cabrillo viewed it in 1542. Today, it is home to both the Port of Los Angeles, the nation's busiest port, and the Port of Long Beach, the second-busiest. The area's amazing transformation began with two outstanding men. The first was Phineas Banning, who envisioned a great harbor here soon after arriving by ship from Delaware in 1853. Banning subsequently built a fleet of boats to ferry cargo and travelers to and from ships anchored offshore. He constructed wharves and warehouses and organized a transportation company that shuttled people and wares between the port and the city 22 miles away. He also founded the town of Wilmington and, in 1869, connected both the port and town with L.A.'s first railway.

The second man, Senator Stephen M. White, led a campaign in the 1890s to obtain federal funds to build a breakwater that would lead to the creation of the city-owned port in San Pedro Bay. When Congress approved those funds, the powerful Southern Pacific Railroad's rival plan to build a private port in Santa Monica Bay was scrapped. In April 1899, thousands of people from Wilmington, San Pedro, and the City of Los Angeles celebrated with a two-day "Free Harbor Jubilee."

City authorities overcame the difficulty of San Pedro Bay's location 22 miles south of the city by annexing the bayside towns of Wilmington and San Pedro and adding a narrow "shoestring" strip linking them with the rest of Los Angeles. After a century of development, the port now encompasses 7,500 acres of land and water, more than 40 miles of waterfront, some 30 cargo terminals, and a busy cruise center. Together with the adjacent Port of Long Beach, the port complex handles up to 8,000 ships carrying all sorts of cargo every year. About half of the goods received at the ports goes to Southern California, with the rest sent across the country.

Both ports have marinas for pleasure craft and offer boat tours along the channels. Long Beach is the proud home of the *Queen Mary* ocean liner, which is open for tours and dining. Visitors who stroll along the promenade south of L.A. Port's cruise center, or who visit the Ports of Call shopping village or dine at restaurants along the main channel, can watch huge container ships and floating hotels pass from just a few hundred feet away.

Los Angeles International Airport

Blessed with extraordinarily fair weather and eager to try almost anything new, Angelenos were among the first in the nation to take to the air. In January 1910, on a makeshift airfield about 10 miles from today's international airport, they erected grandstands to hold some 20,000 people who came each day to witness the first successful air show in the United States. During the ten-day meet, French aviator Louis Paulhan set both a new altitude record (4,164 feet) and an endurance record (64 miles in one hour and 50 minutes), and he took home $14,000 in prize money.

In the aviation craze that followed, Donald Douglas founded the first area aircraft plant in 1915, and neighboring Glendale established the first municipal airport in California in 1923. Five years later, after considering 12 locations for an official city airport, Los Angeles selected a 640-acre parcel about 15 miles southwest of downtown. Since the representing realtor's name was William W. Mines, the airport was known as Mines Field until it was renamed Los Angeles Airport in 1941. In 1949, it became Los Angeles International Airport (LAX).

Today, Los Angeles International Airport is ranked the world's fifth-busiest passenger airport. The 3,500-acre facility has four parallel runways, each monitored by separate controllers from a modern, 277-foot control tower. The most unique structure at the airport is the space-age Theme Building, which boasts a circular restaurant from which diners have great views of planes arriving and departing from the city. Designed by a team of architects that included William Pereira, Welton Becket, and Paul R. Williams, the Theme Building was completed in 1961 and designated an L.A. City Historic-Cultural Monument. Descending to the airport at night over a seemingly endless carpet of lights is widely agreed to be the best way to arrive in L.A.

Art and Ideas

Watts Towers

Long before downtown Los Angeles began sprouting high-rise office towers, a group of lacy spires rose five miles south of downtown, in the working-class community of Watts. The tallest three towers soar 55, 97, and 99 feet into the air, but the structure is actually a complex of 17 individual sculptural works.

The sculptures were single-handedly constructed by an Italian immigrant, Sabbatino "Simon" Rodia. Rodia so loved America that he spent nearly 35 years, from 1921 to 1955, building them as a tribute to his adopted country. He called the work *Nuestro Pueblo*, "our town." Wearing only a window-washer's safety belt and buckle, and using only basic hand tools, Rodia began by constructing a framework of cast-off steel pipes and rod. This he wrapped with chicken wire and covered with a coating of mortar, into

which he pressed broken pieces of pottery, tile, glass, shells, and other random objects. Many of the objects were contributed by neighborhood children or collected by Rodia as he strolled along the nearby Pacific Electric Railway tracks. In 1955, Rodia suddenly moved to northern California where, ten years later, he died in obscurity. Without the creator's presence, Rodia's masterpiece fell into disrepair, only to be saved by a group of artists and preservationists in 1959.

Located in the 1700 block of East 107th Street, the towers are managed today by the Los Angeles City Cultural Affairs Department for the California State Parks. For many, they are a visual symbol of the spirit of freedom and individuality that defines L.A., and they are one of only nine works of folk art on the National Register of Historic Places.

Previous page: the Powell Library on the UCLA campus.

The Huntington Library, Art Collections, and Botanical Gardens

Located northeast of downtown in the community of San Marino, the Huntington, as locals call it, is one of the great treasures of Southern California. Henry E. Huntington, nephew of Collis P. Huntington of Central Pacific Railroad fame, moved to Los Angeles in 1902 and proceeded to turn the local Pacific Electric Railway into the largest interurban railway system in the world. His profits didn't come from fares, but from developing and selling properties along the routes to newcomers who continually poured into Los Angeles County. After selling the railway in 1910, Huntington devoted his energy to expanding his botanical gardens and collecting British and American paintings, furnishings, rare books, and manuscripts. He married his uncle's widow, Arabella, herself a noted art collector, and in 1919 the couple transferred their 200-acre estate and collections to the non-profit trust that operates the Huntington today.

Inside the Lois and Robert F. Erburu Gallery.

The property's newly restored Beaux Arts home displays Henry and Arabella's European art collections (Gainsborough's "Blue Boy" and Lawrence's "Pinkie" are favorites), and the modern Boone Gallery features temporary exhibitions. After remodeling, the Scott and Erburu galleries will house the Huntington's collection of American art. Eye-popping items from the paper archives (such as the double-elephant folio edition of *Audubon's Birds of America*, a Gutenberg Bible, and original Shakespearean and American manuscripts) are on display in the library. The Huntington's museums are set amidst nearly 120 acres of sweeping lawns and immaculately tended specialized gardens, including particularly outstanding Japanese and desert gardens. Due to join them soon is a privately financed, 12-acre traditional Chinese garden, one of the largest outside China.

The Getty Center

Occupying 110 acres of a Los Angeles hilltop, the Richard Meier-designed Getty Center is a comprehensive arts complex that includes the Getty Trust, the J. Paul Getty Museum, the Getty Conservation Institute, the Getty Research Institute, and the Getty Foundation, as well as a restaurant, cafe, garden, and spectacular views stretching from the San Gabriel Mountains to the Pacific Ocean. The $1 billion center was funded entirely from the fortune left by oil magnate and art collector J. Paul Getty, whose trust—the world's largest devoted to art—reached $5.8 billion in 2007. Getty was born in Minneapolis in 1892 but grew up in Los Angeles. His oil company was based in L.A., and his Pacific Palisades Ranch House served as the first J. Paul Getty Museum.

To reach the center, visitors must board a tram at the bottom of the hill. As the tram climbs higher and higher, it gives one time to prepare for the experience that begins on arrival at the spacious Getty Center plaza. Some people visit the center mainly to study Richard Meier's Modernist architecture, which here features rough-hewn blocks of Italian travertine, sweeping metal curves, and a network of terraces. Many start at the J. Paul Getty Museum, which consists of five buildings surrounding a courtyard, while others head for the winding, streamside garden path that leads down to the circular Central Garden designed by artist Robert Irwin.

The museum houses European paintings, drawings, sculpture, illuminated manuscripts, decorative arts, and European and American photographs. Dynamic changing exhibitions also take place year-round. A recent addition to the museum is a collection of modern sculptures donated by the estate of film producer Ray Stark and his wife Fran. A new garden at the lower tram station features many of these works.

The Getty Villa

Set on a coastal bluff just south of Malibu, the Getty Villa is an L.A. cultural icon. The original structure, which opened in 1974 as the J. Paul Getty Museum, was modeled after an ancient Roman country house in Herculaneum, a city that was buried with Pompeii during the 79 A.D. eruption of Mt. Vesuvius. The museum was built to display the antiquities, European paintings, decorative arts, and drawings collected by J. Paul Getty, an oil magnate and entrepreneur and the richest man in the world at the time. When the Getty Center opened in 1997, the villa closed for a much-needed expansion and renovation, reopening in January 2006.

The Getty Villa is acclaimed as having one of the finest collections of ancient Greek, Roman, and Etruscan arts in the nation. Highlights include the Getty Bronze, a nearly 5-foot-tall statue of a young Greek athlete fashioned some time between 300 and 100 B.C., and the Lansdowne Herakles, a 6-foot 4-inch Roman representation of the Greek hero, sculpted in marble about A.D. 125. Works at the villa are arranged thematically in 23 light-filled galleries. Six other galleries feature changing exhibits from the museum's 44,000-piece collection as well as works on loan.

Recent additions at the villa include a stunning array of rare ancient works in glass and the mummy of a young man wearing a gold wreath. A new space has also been designed for conservation and education, and the Ranch House, which once served as Getty's residence and original museum, now contains a 20,000-volume research library. Also new are an outdoor amphitheater, a family room with hands-on activities for children, and the TimeScape Room, featuring interactive explorations of the ancient Mediterranean world.

Los Angeles County Museum of Art

The Los Angeles County Museum of Art, or LACMA for short, is one of America's largest and most comprehensive art museums. Located on Wilshire Boulevard in a district known as Museum Row, it is a major cultural destination for residents and visitors. The museum's permanent collection contains more than 150,000 individual works, with the strongest holdings in Japanese, Islamic, and ancient Near Eastern arts. The museum also hosts major traveling exhibits and offers wide-ranging educational and entertainment programs.

Compared to museums in older cities, LACMA got off to a late start. It was officially created as part of the Los Angeles Museum of History, Science, and Art, but when that museum opened in 1913, the only art on display was borrowed. As the city grew, however, so did its art collection, and in 1965 LACMA opened as an independent entity. The museum began as three separate buildings, but has gone through a series of renovations and expansions, adding three structures, including a distinctive Pavilion for Japanese Art and, half a block away, a former 1940s department store repurposed as LACMA West.

LACMA is now in the midst of an ambitious transformation to expand gallery space and improve visitor access and flow. The first phase is already complete, with a new main entrance and orientation area designed by Italian architect Renzo Piano, as well as a new underground garage, a covered concourse linking the far ends of the grounds, and the new 60,000-square-foot Broad Museum of Contemporary Art. New outdoor sculptures and huge colorful wall hangings have also given LACMA a more colorful, modern look.

University of Southern California

Los Angeles was still a horse-and-buggy town with dirt streets and gas lamps in 1880, when the University of Southern California (USC) opened its doors to 53 students and 10 instructors. The oldest private university in the West, USC was founded by the Methodist Episcopal Church on land donated by an ecumenical trio consisting of a Catholic, a Protestant, and a Jew. The school now has about 33,000 pre- and post-graduate students and 3,200 full-time faculty members.

The 226-acre University Park campus, located directly north of Exposition Park, is home to the College of Letters, Arts and Sciences, the Graduate School, and 15 of 17 professional schools, including the Marshall School of Business, Annenberg School for Communication, Thornton School for Music, and the country's oldest, highly acclaimed School of Cinematic Arts. One of the newer buildings, adjacent to the 110 Freeway, is the handsome Galen Center for basketball, volleyball, and special events. The Doheny Memorial Library and the Widney Alumni House, a California Historic Landmark, are in the center of the park-like campus. The university's Keck School of Medicine and Pharmacology is located across town, near L.A.'s landmark County Hospital.

Academics aside, what distinguishes USC for many is Trojan football. The team has remained the dominant collegiate team in the West since it was organized in 1888 to—what else?—raise money for the university. The team has a truly impressive résumé, including, as of 2007, 11 national football championships and more players sent to the NFL than from any other college or university.

Galen Center.

Norton Simon Museum of Art

Below: Visitors at the Norton Simon Museum.

Opposite above: A view of the Norton Simon Museum's Renaissance gallery.

Opposite below: Visitors in the Norton Simon Museum's Impressionist gallery.

Set behind a brown tile wall and dark green vegetation at the corner of Colorado Street and Orange Grove Boulevard in Pasadena, the Norton Simon Museum of Art contains one of the finest collections of European, American, and Asian art in the United States. The museum was founded by billionaire industrialist Norton Simon, who took over the troubled Pasadena Art Museum in 1974 and merged it with his own superior collection. The museum's treasures now include 14 paintings and pastels by Edgar Degas, as well as 36 bronze statues of dancers cast from Degas' original waxes. Also on view are master paintings by Van Gogh, Cezanne, Manet, Zuraban, Watteau, and Popova, plus works from the Galka E. Scheyer Collection of Blue Four artists: Kandinsky, Klee, Fenninger, and Jawlensky. All are displayed in galleries sensitively designed by architect Frank Gehry, who also redesigned the central garden. Changing exhibits and many of the museum's Asian treasures are presented on the lower level.

Museum of Contemporary Art

Above: MOCA Grand Avenue by architect Arata Isozaki.

Opposite above: Installation view of Skin + Bones: Parallel Practices in Fashion and Architecture at MOCA Grand Avenue, 2006.

Opposite below: Installation view of Ecstasy: In and About Altered States at The Geffen Contemporary at MOCA, 2005.

For most of the twentieth century, Los Angeles was the only major city in the U.S. without a museum of modern art. In fact, it wasn't until Californians passed the 1978 anti-tax Proposition 13—killing proposals for a modern-art addition to the LACMA—that private individuals took up the cause, raising the funds and making the deals that resulted in the opening of the Museum of Contemporary Art (MOCA) in 1986.

Now widely praised as one of the finest collections of post-1940 visual arts in the world, the museum occupies three quite different venues. The main building, at 250 S. Grand Avenue, was designed by Pritzker Prize–winning Japanese architect Arata Isozoki, with part of the structure above ground and part below. The visible portion is a combination of pyramids, cylinders, and cubes featuring hand-cut, laser-polished red sandstone from India, dark-green aluminum cross-hatched in pink, and copper and glass. Inside, the building has 24,000 square feet of well-lit gallery space.

The second venue, located behind the Japanese American National Museum in Little Tokyo, was actually the first to be finished. Opened in 1981 as the "Temporary Contemporary," the 45,000-square-foot former warehouse was remodeled by Frank Gehry to serve as a temporary venue until the Grand Avenue museum could be completed. But the space proved

so popular that its original $1-a-year lease was extended to 2038, and the museum was renamed the Geffen Contemporary at MOCA, after entertainment entrepreneur and philanthropist David Geffen. The museum's third location, MOCA at the Pacific Design Center in West Hollywood, features 3,000 square feet of new works and other special exhibits.

The Colburn School

The Colburn School began in 1950 as a preparatory program for the University of Southern California School of Music, but became independent in 1980 thanks to the generosity of entrepreneur Richard D. Colburn. In 1988, the school was renamed in his honor and, in 1998, moved to a new, 55,000-square-foot facility on Grand Avenue, next to the Museum of Contemporary Art and near the Walt Disney Concert Hall and the Music Center. In 2007, 326,000 square feet, including student residences, were added to the original building.

The Colburn offers two highly regarded programs. The School of Performing Arts gives instruction in music, dance, and drama for some 2,200 students age two and older. The Colburn Conservatory of Music provides a small number of college-age and older students with full tuition, room, and board. With its emphasis on performance, the Colburn naturally offers the public a wide range of recitals and concerts, many held in Herbert Zipper Hall, a 415-seat auditorium designed especially for the playing and recording of chamber music.

Herbert Zipper Concert Hall

Also within the Colburn is the relocated studio designed by architect Frank Lloyd Wright for Jascha Heifetz. It was used by the violinist at his Beverly Hills home from 1946 until his death in 1987. Saved from destruction by Richard Colburn and the school, the room now serves as a teaching studio.

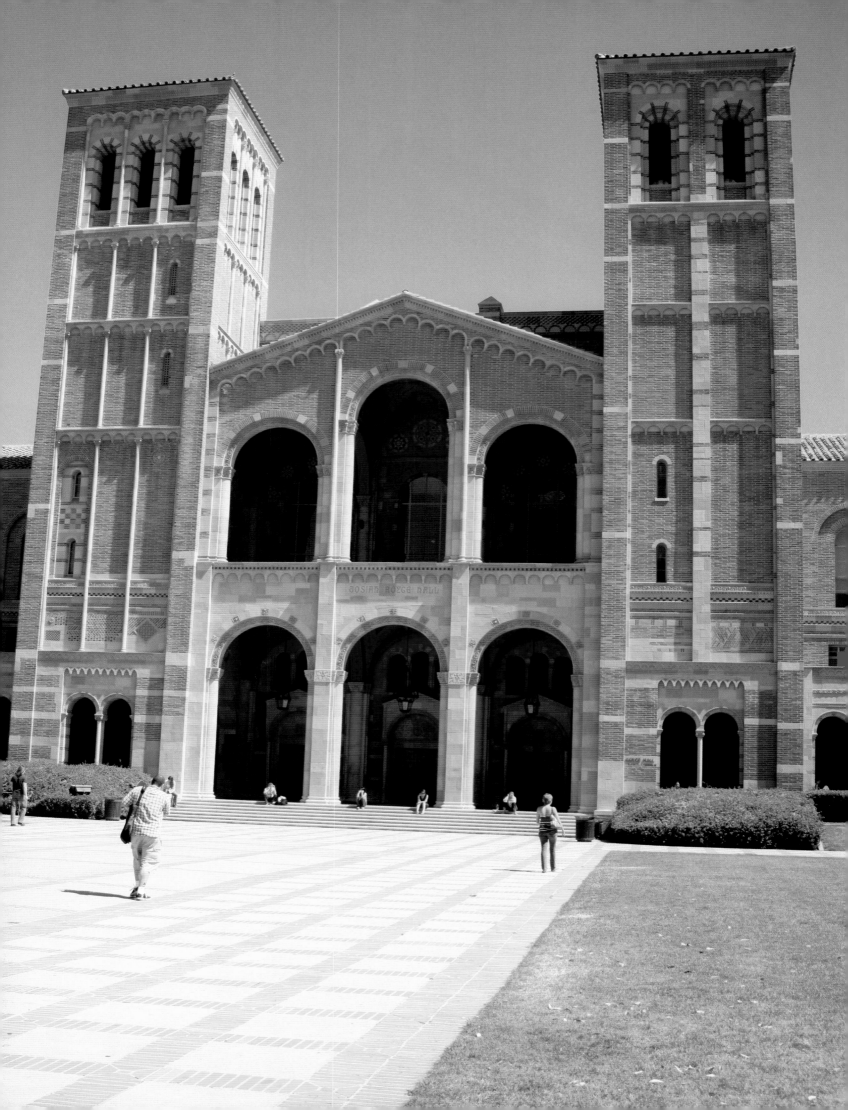

University of California, Los Angeles

The University of California, Los Angeles (UCLA), consistently rated one of the top public universities in the country, began quite humbly in 1882 as a state teacher's college. In 1919, it became the Southern Branch of the University of California and, in order to make way for the new Central Library, moved from its downtown location to Vermont Avenue in East Hollywood. Ten years later, when Royce Hall, Haines Hall, and the Powell Library were completed, the school made a final move to Westwood.

UCLA now consists of at least 175 buildings on a 420-acre campus between Westwood Village and Bel-Air, and serves a student body of about 36,000, approximately three-fifths of them undergrads. In addition to the College of Letters and Sciences, the university has eleven professional schools, including ones for law, public affairs, public health, and theater, film, and televi-

sion. The medical school, established in the 1950s, was renamed for David Geffen after the entertainment entrepreneur and philanthropist made a historic $200 million unrestricted grant in 2002.

When it comes to sports, basketball has been UCLA's strong suit, especially during the reign of Coach John Wooden, when the Bruins won an unprecedented ten NCAA championships, including seven in a row between 1966 and 1973. While the Bruins never built a football powerhouse like that of their cross-town rivals at USC, they did have their own individual stars, including a famous 1940 backfield with Kenny Washington and Jackie Robinson. Rafer Johnson, who thrilled the nation when he brought home the gold in the 1960 Olympic decathlon, was also a product of UCLA. In May 2007, when the women's water polo team claimed victory over Stanford, UCLA became the first school ever to win 100 NCAA team championships.

Opposite:
Royce Hall.

L.A. Murals

One of the distinguishing characteristics of Los Angeles is its amazing array of murals. Well over a thousand can be found throughout the city on the sides of buildings, on bridge supports, or on any other large expanse of concrete. Unfortunately, muralists sometimes have to compete for space with gang taggers, and some wonderful murals have been lost this way. Many still survive though, and new ones are constantly being created.

The first notable mural in the city, *America Tropical*, was painted on an Olvera Street wall in 1932 by David Alfaro Siqueiros, one of the three great Mexican muralists of the twentieth century. Because of its political content, that mural was soon whitewashed over. But Siqueiros' spirit was revived in the late 1960s and early 1970s, when the modern mural movement blossomed with the birth of new social and political movements, particularly the Chicano movement. Los Angeles' large Mexican American population naturally drew on the Mexican mural tradition, expressing pride in their heritage and demands for social justice on walls in East L.A. and other Chicano neighborhoods.

"The Great Wall of Los Angeles" is the largest mural in the city, measuring 2,754 feet (a half mile) in length. Begun in 1974 in a San Fernando Valley flood channel and completed five years later, "The Great Wall" was created by more than 400 young people from various social and economic backgrounds working with artists, oral historians, ethnologists, scholars, and community leaders. Judith F. Baca, then a Boyle Heights art teacher and muralist herself, was instrumental in getting city support for the project. She also helped found the Social and Public Art Resource Center (SPARC) in 1976, an organization that documents, inspects, and maintains L.A.'s murals and provides the public with mural information, maps, and tours.

Let Us Entertain You

Grauman's Chinese Theatre

The most famous of Hollywood's early movie palaces, Grauman's Chinese Theatre is a major destination for most visitors to L.A. Located next to the Hollywood and Highland Center, the theater's main attractions are the handprints and footprints left in the forecourt by nearly 200 of the movie industry's past and present stars. Built in 1927, Grauman's was financed by promoter extraordinaire Sid Grauman and actors Douglas Fairbanks and Mary Pickford. The three were also the first to press their hands in concrete a few days before the

theater opened for the extravagant premiere of Cecil B. DeMille's *The King of Kings*. Unlike Grauman's other theaters—which include the Million Dollar Theater downtown and the Egyptian on Hollywood Boulevard, now home to the American Cinematheque—the 2,200-seat Chinese Theatre still screens first-run films. Although it has been restored, Grauman's retains much of its original beauty and ornamentation, such as the huge chandelier in the auditorium that hangs from an ornate starburst base surrounded by a ring of dragons.

*Previous page: The Chandler Pavilion and Disney Hall, far left,
part of downtown L.A.'s skyline.*

Pantages Theater

The last and most beautiful of the grand movie palaces built in Hollywood, and the last in a national chain developed by Greek immigrant Alexander Pantages, this theater was built at the end of the 1920s with a then-whopping $1.25 million. The dazzling structure opened at the corner of Hollywood Boulevard and Argyle on June 4, 1930. Comedian Eddie Cantor served as master of ceremonies for the evening's entertainment, which featured Marion Davies in *The Floradora Girl* (noted for a rare color sequence), as well as a live revue, an orchestral performance, a jazz band, and the Mickey Mouse cartoon *Cactus Kid*. Because of its rich history and beauty, the Pantages made an excellent venue for the Academy Awards during the 1950s, and for the television Emmys until 1977. Since 2000, however, when the Pantages was restored to its original grandeur for nearly $10 million, the building has hosted mainly theater productions, and is now a particularly popular venue for traveling Broadway shows.

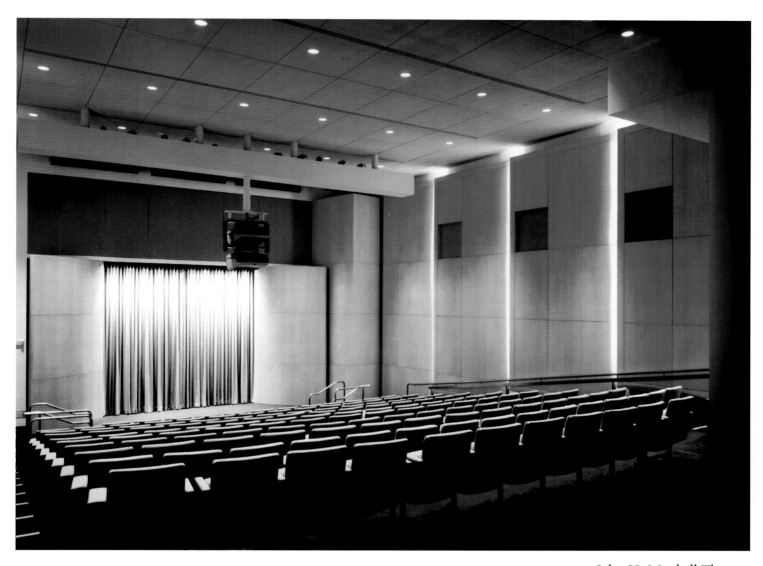

John H. Mitchell Theater.

Paley Center for Media

The Paley Center for Media—formerly known as the Museum of Broadcasting and the Museum of Television and Radio—is named for William S. Paley, the man who purchased the struggling CBS radio network in 1928 and turned it into the highly respected "Tiffany Network" of the 1960s and '70s. Paley personally financed the first museum, which opened in New York City in 1975. In 1996, a second branch opened in Beverly Hills, financed by Los Angeles industry members. Paley's name didn't make it into the title until 2007, when the institution decided that the new name would both honor the original benefactor and better reflect the dramatic technological changes in the delivery of news and entertainment over the past quarter century. The center's leaders were also happy to drop the word "museum," as its collections consist almost exclusively of media archives, not exhibits of objects.

In the beginning, the center's main purpose was to preserve and make available to the public the best radio and television programs in broadcasting history. Now, it focuses more on bringing together media producers and executives to discuss how shows are created and to explore the role of media in society. But its original mission has not been lost entirely: visitors still enjoy coming to watch and listen to some of the 120,000-plus television and radio shows in the archives, or to attend the special screenings and festivals held at the center. For others, it's reward enough just to see and appreciate Richard Meier's stunning Modernist architecture.

Above: Revenge of the Mummy ride.

Opposite: Jurassic Park ride.

Universal Studios

One of the largest producers of feature films, television series, and other forms of entertainment, Universal Studios owes its beginning to Bavarian immigrant Carl Laemmle. Owner of a New York movie company since 1906, Laemmle moved west in 1911 and set up shop as Universal Films across the street from the Nestor Film Company, the first movie studio in Hollywood. A man of bold ideas and grand visions, Laemmle engineered a merger with at least five other companies, forming Universal Pictures. The company moved just a few miles from Universal Films' original site to a 230-acre ranch in the south San Fernando Valley. There, Universal founded its own town, Universal City, and officially opened the new studio in 1915. To help build a market, Laemmle built outdoor stands at the studio so that movie fans could watch the filming, essentially creating the world's first behind-the-scenes "studio tours."

Those "tours" ended when silent films gave way to "soundies," but they made a grand reappearance in the 1960s with the opening of an entire silver screen-inspired theme park called Universal Studios Hollywood. Besides a motorized tour through the studio's sound stages and back lot—where visitors can see the original Psycho House—the park grounds also feature movie-inspired rides, a popular animal show, interactive special-effects stages, and costumed characters from Universal films strolling about. Even visitors without tickets to the park itself can enjoy the Universal City Walk, an adjacent, pedestrian-friendly promenade with shops, restaurants, and theaters.

Hollywood Bowl

Tucked in a canyon off Cahuenga Pass, the Hollywood Bowl is the largest and one of the most successful outdoor venues for classical and popular music in the world. Virtually every top conductor and musician has performed here: Leopold Stokowski, Esa-Pekka Solanen, Frank Sinatra, Pavarotti, Billie Holliday, Barbra Streisand, the Beatles, Miles Davis, James Brown, Monte Python's Flying Circus, and many, many more.

The idea for the Bowl in Hollywood goes back to 1916, when a pageant performance of Shakespeare's "Julius Caesar" drew an estimated 40,000 to nearby Beachwood Canyon. Inspired by the turnout, a group of local culture enthusiasts purchased the natural amphitheater in Cahunga Pass, then known as Daisy Dell, and cleared the brush. By 1918, actors and musicians were performing on a simple wooden stage for folks seated on blankets spread out on the ground. After a 1920 Easter sunrise service on a hilltop in East Hollywood drew another impressive crowd, the Bowl hosted its own first annual sunrise service in 1921. The next year saw the construction of wooden benches and the first annual summer concerts under the stars by the Los Angeles Philharmonic.

Over the decades, the band shell and seating have been redesigned numerous times. The Bowl now seats 18,000, but its record attendance is 26,410, a crowd attracted by French opera star Lily Pons in 1936. The grounds, which are open daily, include a museum with exhibits illustrating the Bowl's fascinating, star-studded history.

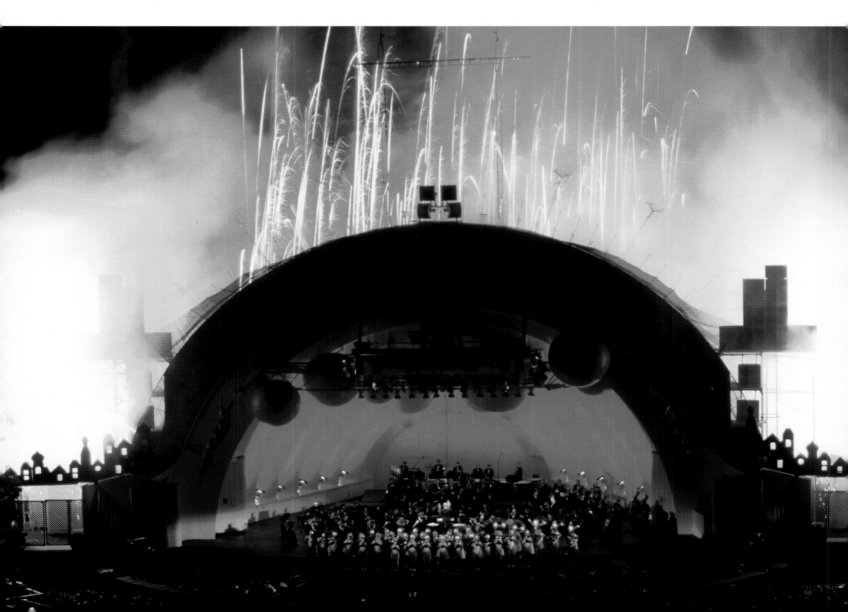

Capitol Records Tower

Looking to some like a stack of 45-rpm records topped by a stylized needle, the Capitol Records building on Vine Street near Hollywood Boulevard is one of the defining landmarks of Hollywood and Los Angeles. The tower's design is credited to Welton Becket, one of the premier architects of mid-century L.A., although Becket reportedly said the cylindrical shape was the idea of his staff member Louis Naidorf. When the building was first occupied, a blinking light on top began spelling out the word "Hollywood" in Morse code, and continues to do so to this day.

The tower was built between 1954 and 1956 to house the offices and studios of the first modern music-recording studio on the West Coast. Capitol Records was founded in 1942 by songwriter Johnny Mercer, movie producer Buddy DeSylva, and record store-owner Glenn Wallichs. Their performers' roster grew to include Frank Sinatra, Judy Garland, and Nat "King" Cole. Since 1955, it has been owned by the English recording company EMI, the Beatles' first recording label.

Left: An orchestra plays Tchaikovsky's 1812 Overture at Los Angeles' Hollywood Bowl with blazing fireworks providing the percussion.

Music Center

The Music Center began as the dream of Dorothy Buffum Chandler, wife of Norman Chandler, publisher of the Los Angeles *Times* from 1945 to 1960, and mother of Otis Chandler, the paper's publisher from 1960 to 1980. Mrs. Chandler was determined that Los Angeles should have a first-rate performance center, one that would reflect the city's growing status in the 1950s. With the help of wealthy friends and institutions, she raised $18.5 million in cash and another $13.7 million in bonds to construct not one but *three* venues on the highest spot of downtown's newly redeveloped Bunker Hill. In December 1964, the 3,297-seat Dorothy Chandler Pavilion opened as the new home of the Los Angeles Philharmonic Orchestra, and as a theater for opera and dance as well. Three years later, the 745-seat Mark Taper Forum and the 1,600-seat Ahmanson Theater completed the center, which has remained the cultural heart and soul of Los Angeles.

Bounded by Grand Avenue and Temple, First, and Hope streets, the Music Center was designed by the local firm of Welton Becket, whose works also include the Capitol Records Tower, Century City, and UCLA's Pauley Pavilion and Schoenberg Hall. Besides the many thousands who come each year to enjoy the music, dance, and theater, many others come to the center for its great views of City Hall and the surrounding area, or just to relax on the wide plaza, with its playful water fountain surrounding the "Peace on Earth" sculpture, one of the last works of Jacques Lipchitz.

Opposite: The Dorothy Chandler Pavilion.

Walt Disney Concert Hall

In 1987, Walt Disney's widow, Lillian, donated $50 million toward a new, world-class performance space for Los Angeles. Sixteen years later, after a series of construction delays, design modifications, and further funding campaigns, the $270 million-plus Walt Disney Concert Hall opened to rave reviews. One critic declared the Frank Gehry-designed work "a vanguard masterpiece." Another delighted in the way the structure's stainless-steel exterior burst up from the site "with a sort of mad exuberance," spilling out "like the petals of an exotic flower."

The apparent lack of any square corners in the hall's interior took some time to earn approval. But praise was immediate and universal for the 2,265-seat auditorium, whose curves and bows place the audience's focus totally on the performers. Clad in honey-colored Douglas fir and stepped with fourteen sharply raked seating sections that completely surround the stage, the room has an incredibly warm, even cozy feel that makes attending a musical performance here a communal experience. The all-important acoustics are among the finest in the world, and the 6,125-pipe organ, with a Gehry-designed splay of pipes—which some initially likened to a stack of French fries—is a wonder to see as well as hear. Located on First Street across from the Dorothy Chandler Pavilion, the now-beloved concert hall is home to the Los Angeles Philharmonic Orchestra and the Master Chorale.

Knott's Berry Farm

Knott's Berry Farm, now one of the most popular amusement parks in America, began as an actual working farm that became a favorite stop for travelers driving to and from Los Angeles. During the 1930s, folks began pulling over here to buy the unique boysenberries that a local horticulturist, Rudolph Boysen, had created by crossing blackberries, red raspberries, and loganberries. Boysen failed to turn a profit on his berries, but farmer Walter Knott nursed the abandoned plants back to life, and his wife Cordelia started selling boysenberry preserves as well as the fresh berries at a roadside stand. By 1940, the farm also had a restaurant famed for Cordelia's fried chicken and boysenberry pie dinners. Walter Knott then added a make-believe Old West town, where the tinkle of nickelodeons was occasionally interrupted by bangs from an impromptu dramatized gunfight. By the time Disneyland opened nearby in 1956, Knott's was already Southern California's first theme park.

Although Walter and Cordelia Knott passed away long ago, Knott's Berry Farm remains a popular family destination. It still has great chicken dinners, but now the 160-acre park also includes a Ghost Town section with one of the best wooden roller coasters in the country—the most popular ride at the park—a Boardwalk area that includes six rides with names like Rip Tide, Boomerang, and Perilous Plunge; Camp Snoopy, with fun rides for youngsters; and Fiesta Village, whose six rides include Montezuma's Revenge and Dragon Swing.

Disneyland

It's said that Walt Disney first got the idea for Disneyland on a visit with his children to Griffith Park. There, the master storyteller found himself wishing there was a park that could be enjoyed equally by adults and children. Disney's deeply creative mind and impressive business savvy turned that wish into an entire world of fun and fantasy in July 1955, when he opened the world's first fully realized theme park on a former Anaheim orange grove.

The original Disneyland contained five "lands": Main Street USA, Adventureland, Frontierland, Fantasyland, and Tomorrowland. The park has since expanded from 45 to 85 acres and added three new "lands": New Orleans Square, Mickey's Toontown, and Critter Country. In 2001, the Walt Disney Company opened an adjacent park, California Adventure, which seeks to entertain and inform visitors about the state's natural and manmade treasures. Famously billed as "the happiest place on earth," the original Disneyland has managed to maintain its popularity for more than 50 years, even replicating itself in Florida, Japan, France, and Hong Kong.

Dodger Stadium

Thousands of Brooklyn hearts were broken in 1957 when Walter O'Malley announced that the Dodgers baseball team, based in Brooklyn since 1890 and playing on Ebbets Field since 1913, would be leaving for a brand new stadium in—of all places!—Los Angeles. Development of the stadium site required the forcible eviction of the last remaining Mexican American residents in the canyon named Chavez Ravine and the abandonment of plans for a new public housing project there. But the Dodgers came, beginning a westward movement of pro baseball, football, and hockey teams that forever changed the landscape of professional sports in and beyond Los Angeles.

While Dodger Stadium was under construction, the team played its first four seasons in L.A. at the Memorial Coliseum. The new stadium was christened April 10, 1962, unfortunately with a loss to the Cincinnati Reds. But that game was followed by two wins over the Reds, and a record 102 wins for the season. For their first three years, the Dodgers shared their stadium with the Los Angeles Angels, the new American League baseball franchise. In addition to baseball games, the arena has also hosted rock and pop concerts and many other kinds of events, including a mass by Pope John Paul II in 1987.

Set on a flattened hilltop next to Elysian Park, Dodger Stadium is surrounded by 21 terraced parking lots that can accommodate 16,000 cars. The arena itself was originally designed to hold 56,000 fans, but the seating has been rearranged somewhat to allow for luxury suites on the club level and traditional box seats along the baselines. The stadium also boasts spectacular views of nearby downtown from the south parking lots and views of the San Gabriel Mountains from the top grandstands.

Sunset Strip

From downtown Los Angeles to Pacific Coast Highway, Sunset Boulevard travels through some of the most distinctive neighborhoods in the county. But the boulevard's most famous section by far is the 1.7-mile-long stretch that winds along the southern slope of the Santa Monica Mountains, known as the Sunset Strip.

In the 1920s, when it was policed by the relatively lenient county sheriff instead of the LAPD, the Strip was known for its speakeasies and gambling dens. But the venerable Sunset Plaza development, the legendary Chateau Marmont hotel, and the beautiful Art Deco Sunset Tower apartments also went up on the boulevard during that decade. The Strip took a really glamorous turn in the next two decades, when Hollywood stars and powerbrokers turned out dressed to the nines to dine at the Vendome and Restaurante La Rue, and to have their photos snapped at fancy nightclubs like the Trocadero and Ciro's. Modest office buildings also began to rise along the Strip to serve talent agents, record company executives, and other company-town players, many of whom lived in nearby hillside homes.

After the 1950s, the Strip became more youthful and democratic, eventually passing through the whole gamut of American pop- and counter-culture phases, from the flower-power 1960s through the go-go and disco-driven '70s, punk rock '80s, grunge '90s, and the twenty first-century's glam and hip-hop musical styles. Music still dominates the Strip, as it has for the past half century. L.A.'s club culture is today centered farther east, in Hollywood, but famed Sunset Strip venues such as the Whisky, the Roxy, and the House of Blues remain key attractions.

Guard Kobe Bryant flying high at a Lakers home game.

Staples Center and L.A. Live

Since opening in 1999, Staples Center has been the only arena in the country serving as home to five professional sports teams: the NBA Lakers and Clippers, the WNBA Sparks, the NHL Kings, and the AFL Avengers. The center has also been a major venue for concerts, ice shows, and boxing and wrestling matches, and it even hosted the Democratic national convention in 2000. Located just off the 110 Freeway, the building's sweeping curves, expanses of glass, and lacquered sheet metal were deliberately chosen by architect Tom Turner to suggest energy and excitement, and to harmonize with the entryway of the adjacent L.A. Convention Center.

Staples Center is part of a still-emerging $2.5 billion sports and entertainment district known as L.A. Live. The ambitious idea for the district was developed by a wholly owned subsidiary of the Anschutz Company, founded by Denver multi-billionare Phillip Anschutz, and designed in part by the international firm RTKL (whose staff now includes Staples Center's architect, Tom Turner). L.A. Live will ultimately include the 7,100-seat Nokia Theatre for music and dramatic programs; a 54-story, 1,000-room hotel and condominium complex operated by J. W. Marriott and the Ritz-Carlton, with the top 26 floors dedicated to condos priced at $1.5 to $6 million; a 2,200-capacity Club Nokia for live music; a 40,000-square-foot retail plaza featuring giant LED screens; and multiple movie screens. The multi-phase project aims to present a glittery challenge to New York's Times Square and Tokyo's Ginza.

A Home for Science
and Technology

California Science Center

The California Science Center is a wonderful place to introduce curious minds to the worlds of science and technology. The center is the third state exhibit hall to occupy the Exposition Park site. The first, built in 1912, displayed agricultural products, which were so important to L.A.'s economy at the time. The second, the California Museum of Science and Industry, focused on the new knowledge and technologies during its period of tenure, from 1951 to 1998. The current center is a state-of-the-art science education facility housed in a modern, nearly all-new glass and concrete building.

Interactive displays dominate the permanent exhibits, whose titles are "The World of Life" and "The Creative World." The center also includes an IMAX theater dedicated to science-oriented films, a refurbished Air and Space Gallery, and a well-displayed B2 Stealth Bomber. Two other facilities at the center are not open to the general public: a science charter school and the Amgen Center for Science Learning, a resource and training center for science teachers and professionals. Due to be finished in 2009 is a major, 170,000-square-foot pavilion dedicated to "The World of Ecology," with live animals and plants and 175 interactive exhibits.

Natural History Museum of Los Angeles County

With all the kinetic energy in and around the adjacent California Science Center, it can be comforting to step inside the cool, high-ceilinged, marble-floored Natural History Museum, one of many National Historic Places in L.A. The museum opened November 6, 1913, one day after dedication of the Owens Valley Aqueduct at the Cascades. Back then, the institution was called the Los Angeles Museum of History, Science, and Art, and its building consisted of a central rotunda and three wings, one for each subject in its name. The only entryway was from the still-popular rose garden at the east end of the building. Now, after a series of expansions, visitors enter either from the south side that faces the Los Angeles Memorial Coliseum, or from the north, which looks toward the University of Southern California campus.

The art part of the museum left in the 1960s to become the Los Angeles County Museum of Art, leading trustees to change the name to include just science and history. Today, the museum houses more than 33 million indi-vidual objects, making it one of the largest museums of natural and cultural history in the United States. Highlights include three huge halls with lifelike African and North American dioramas; a large dinosaur exhibit featuring a complete skeleton of a Mamenchisaurus, the longest-necked dinosaur yet discovered; and a gem and mineral hall boasting one of the world's largest gold exhibits. In the cultural area, the museum has an extensive California history section that traces L.A.'s past from pre-history through the 1940s. Especially for youngsters is the Discovery Room, which offers hands-on science activities and close-up encounters with live, creepy-crawly creatures.

The museum has recently completed a major seismic refit and restoration, bringing the terra-cotta gargoyles, mosaic floors, and stained-glass skylights of the original structure back to their original luster. Future improvements include a new hall of dinosaurs that will display Thomas, one of the most complete Tyrannosaurus rex dinosaurs ever discovered.

Aquarium of the Pacific

With nearly 1,000 species and more than 12,500 inhabitants, the Aquarium of the Pacific has been the largest facility of its kind in Southern California since it opened in 1998. Located off Shoreline Drive in Long Beach, the aquarium greets visitors with a three-story–high tank that brings even the shortest tot only inches away from the sharks, barracudas, and other Pacific predators inside. From there, the exhibits are divided into three main sections. One is dedicated to the temperate waters of Southern California and neighboring Baja California. The Northern Pacific section includes Puffins, a giant Pacific octopus, and other cold-water creatures. The Tropical Pacific section features a 350,000-gallon tank full of colorful reef fish, as well as smaller enclosures for sea horses, sea dragons, and other fanciful warm-water creatures. Outdoor exhibits include a Lorikeet Forest, where visitors can hand-feed the parakeet-like birds from Australia, and a Shark Lagoon that allows daring youngsters—and adults—a chance to touch the wildlife. There's also a play area for children, a theater, and great views of the *Queen Mary* ocean liner moored across the bay.

California Institute of Technology

Caltech, as the California Institute of Technology is known, occupies a relatively small and unassuming campus in a residential area of East Pasadena. But its size and looks are deceiving, as Caltech is one of the finest research and educational institutions in the world. As of 2007, faculty members had received 32 Nobel Prizes, and their discoveries and inventions have had enormous impact on the modern world and on our understanding of our place in the universe.

Founded in 1891 as Throop University by a retired Chicago businessman and politician, the school offered classes in arts, crafts, and teacher training until 1907, when the acclaimed astronomer George Ellery Hale became a trustee. Hale had also come west from Chicago, in 1903, to establish the Mt. Wilson Observatory overlooking Pasadena. That observatory dominated the study of astronomy worldwide through the first half of the twentieth century. Under his guidance, the school dropped all classes except science and technology, and Hale raised the funds

needed and recruited the two men who would lead the school into the future.

Those two men were chemist and former MIT president Arthur Amos Noyes and experimental physicist Robert Andrews Millikan, both Nobel laureates. During the 1920s and '30s, Noyes and Millikan expanded the newly renamed California Institute of Technology into new research areas. The list of discoveries made at the school during their tenure include that of anti-matter, the nature of the chemical bond, the foundations of molecular biology, and the birth of modern earthquake science. It was also early experiments in rocketry by a handful of Caltech students that led to the founding of the Jet Propulsion Laboratory, whose unmanned explorations have taken us to the moon and Mars and revealed many of the secrets of our universe and beyond. Albert Einstein spent two months in 1931, 1932, and 1933 consulting with Caltech scientists about his general theory of relativity while also enjoying the California sunshine and meeting Hollywood stars.

Opposite: Beckman Auditorium on the Caltech campus.

Jet Propulsion Laboratory

Since 1958, the Jet Propulsion Laboratory (JPL) has been designing and operating nearly all U.S. unmanned explorations of the moon and planets in our solar system. Funded by the National Aeronautics and Space Administration (NASA) and managed by the California Institute of Technology (Caltech), JPL occupies a 177-acre site on the western edge of the Arroyo Seco, not far from where a few Caltech students performed the mid-1930s rocket experiments that eventually led to the lab's founding.

The term "Jet Propulsion Laboratory" first appeared in a 1943 Caltech proposal to develop a missile for the U.S. Army Air Corps in response to Germany's V-2 rocket. In 1949, the lab succeeded in sending a reconstructed V-2 rocket 244 miles above the earth. This first U.S. entry into space launched the new "aerospace" industry, with Los Angeles as its leader. For the next eight Cold War years, JPL focused on designing bigger and better missiles, until October 1957, when Russia shocked the U.S. with its successful launch of Sputnik, Earth's first manmade satellite.

After that amazing feat, JPL turned its attention from designing rockets to designing the objects that rockets put into orbit. Since the January 1958 launch of Explorer 1, the first U.S. satellite, the lab has placed robotic craft on the moon and Mars, and sent orbiters or flybys to Venus, Neptune, Jupiter, Saturn, and Uranus. It's also sent equipment to the International Space Station and repaired the Hubble Space Telescope. In recent years, JPL has often turned its eyes back to earth, studying how clouds affect our weather and water and keeping tabs on ozone levels, changes in artic sea ice, and rising temperatures. The lab has even used satellites to help locate hidden ancient cities and developed a camera that helps surgeons map the brain.

Opposite: Aerial View of the Jet Propulsion Laboratory.

Above: View of the L.A. basin from Griffith Observatory.

Griffith Observatory

Sitting high on the southeastern slope of the Santa Monica Mountains, the Griffith Observatory is one of the most visible landmarks in Los Angeles. The idea for a public observatory came from Griffith J. Griffith, who first donated some of his Rancho Los Feliz land for a public park in 1896, and later gave the city $100,000 to build an observatory and a Greek theater in it. Unfortunately, plans for the observatory did not begin for another 30 years, because the gift came shortly after Griffith scandalized city fathers by wounding his wife in an attempted murder. Griffith went to jail and proved a model inmate, but his money was placed in a trust until 1931, well after Griffith and the memory of his deed had passed. By the time it was released, the trust had grown to $750,000.

The park's Greek Theatre was completed first, opening in 1929, and the observatory followed in 1935. Best known by some from the movies—most notably the 1955 feature *Rebel Without a Cause* starring James Dean and Natalie Wood—the observatory was designed by local architects John C. Austin and Frederick M. Ashley using Egyptian, Art Deco, and Moderne styles. Over the years, millions of people, including virtually every Los Angeles school child, have come here to get their first real-time view of sunspots, provided by a solar telescope, and to look through the observatory's 12-inch Zeiss refracting telescope at planets, distant stars, and asteroids as they streak past Earth.

After a recent $93 million expansion and renovation, the exterior of the observatory looks just as it did before, only ringed with a new necklace of lights at night. Guests entering through the original front doors (instead of a new lower-level entry) will find the Hugo Ballin murals in the rotunda nicely cleaned, and the Foucault pendulum still hypnotically tracing the earth's rotation in a bed of sand. Also on the first floor is the thrilling Tesla coil and the entrance to the completely refurbished planetarium. A curved walkway with a timeline of the universe leads visitors to a cavernous room ominously named the Gunther Depths of Space. There, a new theater, a huge photo mural of the universe, and dozens of interactive exhibits teach and tantalize young and old alike.

Opposite: The observatory and grounds during the 2002–2006 expansion and renovation.

At Home in L.A.

Above: The Doheny Mansion.

West Adams District

West Adams is one of the oldest neighborhoods in Los Angeles. It was the preferred residential area for many of L.A.'s wealthy from 1880 to the 1920s, when Hancock Park and other upscale developments drew Angelenos west. Located just north of the University of Southern California, the district contains one of the nation's largest collections of historic homes, many of them architecturally distinguished.

After the Supreme Court brought restrictive property covenants to a nominal end in 1948, West Adams became the favored spot for wealthy African Americans, including actress Hattie McDaniel, boxing great Joe Louis, singer Ray Charles, and other celebrities. During the 1950s, when residents of means fled smog-choked central and eastern neighborhoods for the cleaner air on L.A.'s "Westside," the district began to decline. But three decades later, when air quality improved and Westside prices soared, West Adams was rediscovered by historic- and architecturally minded Angelenos, who have been gradually restoring the area's homes to their original beauty ever since.

The most famous West Adams home is the Doheny Mansion, one of several buildings within fenced-in Chester Place. The house is the former residence of L.A. oil magnate Edward L. Doheny and his wife Estelle. Doheny purchased the fully furnished, 22-room house in 1901 for the then-astronomical price of $120,000, and Estelle proceeded to fix it up with a 40-foot Louis

Previous: Private residence in Studio City.

Above: St. Vincent de Paul Catholic Church.

Comfort Tiffany glass dome, a mosaic floor of imported marbles, an elegant Pompeian room, and other pricey upgrades. Refurbished after the 1933 earthquake, the home's exterior took on the look of a French Gothic chateau. Estelle willed the home to the Catholic Archdiocese of Los Angeles for educational purposes, and it passed into their care after her death in 1958. Since then, the home has been operated by Mount St.

Mary's College, which offers occasional tours.

Always open to visitors is the nearby St. Vincent de Paul Catholic Church, located on the corner of West Adams and Figueroa boulevards. The church was built in 1925 with funds donated by Edward Doheny and designed by Los Angeles architect Albert C. Martin. It has been called "the finest example of Churrigueresque architecture in Los Angeles."

Echo Park

One of the most historically rich and diverse neighborhoods in Los Angeles, Echo Park grew up around a park and lake that have charmed Angelenos since the 1890s. Bisected east to west by Sunset Boulevard, the community's clapboard cottages and stucco homes cling to hills with some of the steepest streets and stairways in the city. The neighborhood has long been a favorite of "Eastside" artists, writers, composers, and other creative folks, and is also home to a significant Mexican American population. As with Silver Lake, its more upscale neighbor to the west, Echo Park's restaurants and shops have managed to remain owner-operated and chain-free.

The neighborhood encompasses the community formerly known as Edendale, where William Selig, Mack Sennett, and other filmmakers began shooting Westerns and comedies as early as 1909. The Keystone Kops and Tom Mix movies were shot in Edendale, and Walt Disney moved his animation studio here in the 1930s. Echo Park is also where the legendary evangelist Aimee Semple McPherson brought her Foursquare Gospel ministry in 1918, based in the Angelus Temple since its dedication in 1923. (This is also where she returned to after a scandalous month-long tryst with her radio engineer in 1926.) The landmark temple sits across the street from Echo Park's prime attraction: the park that gave the neighborhood its name. The park and lake are open year-round for relaxing, fishing, and paddleboating, but are most colorful in June, when rare resident lotus plants burst into bloom against the background of the downtown Los Angeles skyline.

The Gamble House

The redwood-shingled Gamble House is one of the finest examples of American Arts and Crafts architecture, and the only one open to the public. The home was built for Procter and Gamble heir David B. Gamble and his wife, who left their Cincinnati home to retire in Pasadena. In 1907, they bought a lot at 4 Westmoreland Place, a short street paralleling Orange Grove Boulevard. To design their new home inside and out, they chose architects Charles and Henry Greene and gave them a virtually unlimited budget.

The Greene brothers were also Ohio-born Pasadena transplants. On their way west in 1893, they stopped by the Chicago World's Fair, where they saw examples of Japanese architecture for the first time. They were already converts to the Arts and Crafts esthetic, an artistic movement of the late nineteenth century that valued hand-made objects and the use of natural materials over factory-produced items. After their experience at the World's Fair, the brothers began incorporating the overlapping roofs and exposed beams of Japanese architecture into their designs. These influences can be seen at the Gamble House, alongside such distinguishing features as exotic woods in the interior, artful wall carvings, and a spectacular leaded-glass front door.

The 8,100-square-foot home was completed in only ten months, but the Gambles did not move in for more than a year, until all the Greene-designed furniture, lamps, rugs, and other furnishings had been put in place. Fortunately, the home remained cared for by the Gamble family until 1966, and was then deeded to the City of Pasadena with the proviso that it be maintained and operated by the University of Southern California School of Architecture. As a result, the Gamble House has remained very much intact and lovingly cared for.

Hollyhock House

Built between 1919 and 1921 on an East Hollywood hilltop, Hollyhock House was originally designed by Frank Lloyd Wright, and was his first commission in Los Angeles. Wright's client, Aline Barnsdall, was an oil heiress and arts patron who envisioned her home as the center of a creative community, with studios and housing for artists, and separate theaters for film and drama. But Barnsdall kept fussing with Wright's plans, and the architect was often away attending to his Imperial Hotel project in Tokyo, leaving his son Lloyd and apprentice Rudolf Schindler (both prominent architects-in-the-making) in charge. Due to delays and high taxes, only Barnsdall's home and two smaller structures on the property were finished before the heiress suddenly decided in 1926 to donate the house and part of the hill to the city, with the intent that the building would become a library and the grounds a public park.

Today, Barnsdall Park includes an active municipal art gallery, theater, and Barnsdall's home, named Hollyhock House for her favorite flower. The

The living room in the first Frank Lloyd Wright–designed home in Los Angeles.

house's exterior is Mayan inspired, with highly stylized representations of hollyhocks. Inside, a number of low-ceilinged hallways lead to expansive rooms, the central courtyard, or one of several exterior gardens. To take advantage of L.A.'s year-round temperate climate, most rooms open to the outdoors, and even the roofs were intended as living spaces. The dining room still has its original table and chairs, and the playroom for Barnsdall's young daughter is a rare early example of glass-on-glass corners. Many rooms feature Wright's signature leaded art glass, but the most dramatic room is the huge vaulted living room, where reproductions of Wright-designed furnishings face a subterranean fireplace topped by a massive Wright-designed bas-relief.

West end: exterior of living room with square water fountain.

Venice Canals

Like many early visitors to L.A., cigarette-manufacturing heir Abbott Kinney fell in love with the city's year-round temperate climate and decided to settle in nearby Sierra Madre in 1890. Kinney was a well-traveled, educated man of the world, and he believed L.A. needed a cultural and recreational center fashioned after the Italian city of Venice. When his Venice of America opened on July 4, 1905, it included 16 miles of canals, complete with imported gondolas and singing gondoliers.

Kinney's vision was grand, but his attempt to bring serious culture to the masses soon gave way to Coney Island-type amusements. Moreover, he did not foresee the coming popularity of autos, which were too wide to travel over the canals' narrow bridges. By 1920, when Kinney died, Venice and its canals had begun a slow slide into decay. Ten were filled in with dirt in 1929, surrounding property values plummeted, and, in 1946, the Pacific Electric trolley stopped service to Venice. All of this was just fine, however, with the artists, musicians, beatniks, and hippies who thrived in ramshackle bungalows along Venice's beachfront and canals.

As L.A.'s population continued to boom, pushing the value of seaside properties ever upward, rediscovery of Venice became inevitable. By the 1990s, homeowners were restoring the historic canal-side cottages, or alternately tearing them down and replacing them with three-story homes as close to the city's size limit as possible. The six canals that survived—all between Washington Avenue, South Venice Boulevard, and Pacific and Ocean avenues—were restored, sidewalks were laid, and bridges were repainted. Today, the Venice Canals once again offer strollers a beautiful and peaceful respite from the hustle and bustle of the city just beyond.

Mulholland Drive

One of the most famous roadways in the world, Mulholland Drive twists and turns 22 miles along the crest of the Santa Monica Mountains between the 101 and the 405 freeways, offering spectacular views of the San Fernando Valley, where nearly two million Angelenos make their home. When it opened on December 27, 1924, the road was christened Mulholland Highway after William Mulholland, who envisioned it as the beginning of a scenic highway that would extend all the way to the Pacific and be open for everyone's enjoyment. However, developers who paid for the first section of the road had a different goal: as one wrote, it was to turn "the barren waste of hills into a beautiful residential area."

The hills along Mulholland Drive are now nearly filled with homes—or, more properly, mansions. But the road itself has grown considerably, now forming just a portion of the 55-mile-long, public Mulholland Scenic Parkway and Corridor. The portion west of the 405 Freeway crosses mostly open land until it nears the end at Leo Carrillo State Beach in Pacific Palisades. Along the way are numerous overlooks with places to park and learn from informational exhibits. The road also travels through the 150,000-acre Santa Monica Mountains National Recreation Area, which has more than 600 miles of hiking and riding trails. The park also has a number of popular attractions, such as Paramount Ranch, where visitors can see the sets used in Paramount's and other studios' popular films and television shows.

Beverly Hills City Hall.

Beverly Hills

Ever since Mary Pickford and Douglas Fairbanks moved here in 1919, Beverly Hills has been home to so many movie stars, and associated with so many films and television series, that it's indisputably the best-known L.A.–area neighborhood. The distinctive look of the city, with its wide curving streets lined with stately palm trees, is largely the work of landscape architect Wilbur D. Cook. Cook laid out the city for the Rodeo Land and Water Company, which began developing Beverly Hills in 1906. The city's name came from Burton Green, Rodeo's head of development, who was inspired by the name of Beverly Farms in Massachusetts.

Visitors to Beverly Hills usually enjoy driving through the beautiful residential streets, possibly stopping for refreshments at the legendary Beverly Hills Hotel, the elegant Peninsula, or the Beverly Wilshire Hotel. But the main Beverly Hills attraction is the shopping, particularly along Rodeo Drive. Although only three blocks long, Rodeo Drive and its side streets are crammed with shops bearing such names as Armani and Gucci, Ralph Lauren and Valentino, Cartier and Tiffany. And if those don't satisfy, Neiman Marcus, Saks Fifth Avenue, and other such upscale stores are nearby, on Wilshire Boulevard.

Opposite: Two Rodeo, a shopping lane just off Rodeo Drive.

Larchmont Village

To outsiders, Los Angeles can appear to be an endless blur of buildings and traffic with little sense of community. But L.A. has always had distinct and vibrant neighborhoods where people living nearby love to gather to shop, talk, and eat. One example is Larchmont Village south of Hollywood, a block-long, tree-shaded section of Larchmont Boulevard stretching between Beverly Boulevard and West First Street. With its owner-run book store, cleaners, one-of-a-kind shops, and nearly a dozen restaurants—many with sidewalk seating—Larchmont Village has often been used in commercials to suggest the Main Street of a typical American small town. Other Los Angeles neighborhood centers include Melrose Avenue between La Brea and Fairfax avenues, where a younger crowd gathers to share food and hip fashion, and Leimert Park in the Crenshaw District, a community that celebrates African American art and music.

Previous page:
Beverly Hills.

Hancock Park

It's been said that G. Allan Hancock, the son and heir of Civil War–era Major Henry Hancock, drilled 71 holes on his Rancho La Brea land between 1905 and 1910—and every single one struck oil. In 1920, three years before donating the 23-acre Hancock Park and its tar pits to Los Angeles County, Hancock began developing one of L.A.'s most prestigious residential districts: also (and confusingly so) named Hancock Park. Bounded by Wilshire, Melrose, Rossmore, and Highland, the neighborhood was one of several subdivisions in the city's fledgling western suburbs. Like some of the other new developments there, Hancock Park appealed to the wealthy, both newcomers to L.A. and native beneficiaries of the city's economic boom of the 1920s.

What set Hancock Park apart was that the lots were large, the streets were paved with concrete, utility poles were placed at the rear of the properties, and houses had to be set back at least 50 feet from the curb—conditions that created a particularly attractive and luxurious atmosphere. Each purchaser had to hire their own architect and builder, but homes were typically two stories high, with a porte cochère for one or more autos, and designed in the Spanish Colonial, Tudor, or other popular styles of the day. Now as then, Hancock Park encompasses the Wilshire Country Club, founded and almost single-handedly funded in 1919 by Hancock. The official home of the mayor of Los Angeles, known as the Getty House, is just a few blocks east, at 605 South Irving Boulevard in Windsor Square, one of the neighborhoods that likes to capitalize on Hancock Park's reputation by referring to itself as "Hancock Park-adjacent."

Opposite: The Mayor of Los Angeles' official residence.

San Fernando Valley

From the mid-1940s to the end of the twentieth century, the image of the typical Los Angeles family home was a Spanish- or ranch-style house with a wide front lawn and a backyard patio (ideally with a pool and barbecue), fronting a tree-shaded street in the San Fernando Valley. Bing Crosby, the popular 1940s crooner, vocalized the dream of many a middle-class family and returning World War II soldier when he sang of making "the San Fernando Valley my home." With a no-money-down policy for veterans and new three-bedroom homes priced at around $12,000, "The Valley," as it came to be called, quickly filled in with communities called by appealing names like Valley Village, Sherman Oaks, Panorama City,

and Woodley Park. Those new homes were soon joined by some of America's first big shopping malls, in North Hollywood and Woodland Hills, for example. By 1960, the population in the valley had already topped one million.

Just 60 years before, at the beginning of the twentieth century, the valley had been mostly empty. The only towns—San Fernando, Pacoima, and Burbank—were in the east end. The rest of the valley was dotted with wheat fields and ranches. The transformation began after 1905, when it was learned that Owens River water would be coming to Los Angeles. To profit from the virtually inevitable development, land speculators—among them Los Angeles *Times*

publisher Harry Chandler—optioned nearly all the empty valley land. They then began selling off parcels to subdividers, who tried to lure homebuyers to new towns such as Van Nuys, North Hollywood, and Owensmouth. In order to share in L.A.'s water bounty, however, valley residents had to vote to be annexed to the City of Los Angeles, which is just what they did in 1915.

Today, the San Fernando Valley is home to nearly 2 million people, almost half the total population of the City of Los Angeles. The area is as ethnically and economically diverse as any in Los Angeles. And despite new high-rise buildings, multiple-resident structures, and McMansions that overwhelm their small lots, one can still drive down tree-shaded neighborhood streets in the valley where families really do live an American dream that dates to the 1940s and '50s.

An International
Hometown

Japanese American National Museum

The first Japanese in Los Angeles came south from San Francisco in the 1890s to escape anti-Asian sentiment. Since that time, Japanese and Japanese Americans have played important roles in the economic and cultural life of the city. They established the first abalone fishing colony off Point Fermin and began the fishing industry in San Pedro Bay. Their commercial gardens supplied much of the city's produce in the first decades of the 1900s, and they developed a Japanese business community downtown that became known as Little Tokyo. Regardless of these contributions, within two months after Japan's attack on Pearl Harbor on December 7, 1941, all 37,000 persons of Japanese descent in Los Angeles County—most of them U.S. citizens—were forced from their homes and sent to internment camps for the duration of World War II. Despite this treatment, many Japanese Americans volunteered to fight for the U.S. and its allies, and their 442nd Regimental Combat Team became the most decorated unit in World War II.

To tell their stories, and to celebrate Japanese culture and the contributions of Japanese to America, a group of interested Angelenos founded the Japanese American National Museum in 1982. The museum opened ten years later in a refurbished former Buddhist temple, the first built in Los Angeles. In 1999, the museum moved just a few steps away to a new, 85,000-square-foot facility designed by San Francisco-born architect Gyo Obata. The permanent exhibit, "Common Ground: The Heart of Community," traces the history of Japanese Americans through photos, films, documents, and memorabilia. It even includes a reclaimed barrack from the Heart Mountain incarceration camp. Changing exhibits focus on other aspects of Japanese American life.

Previous page: Wat Thai Buddhist temple.

Opposite: Docent leading a school tour through the core exhibit, Common Ground: The Heart of Community.

The museum is located at the corner of First Street and Alameda Avenue in Little Tokyo, whose other attractions include numerous shops and restaurants; an enchanting, authentic rooftop Japanese garden at the New Otani Hotel (open to the public); and a monument honoring the legendary Japanese American 442nd Regimental Combat Team. Little Tokyo is liveliest in August, when it hosts the annual Nisei Week celebration and a popular Tofu Festival.

Chinatown

In 1870, 100 years before the most recent wave of Chinese immigrants began settling in the San Gabriel Valley, a vibrant Chinese community already existed in downtown Los Angeles near the old Mexican plaza. Unfortunately, that early Chinatown was leveled to make way for Union Station in the 1930s. A substitute quickly grew up in the roughly 30-block area northwest of Olvera Street, forming another thriving neighborhood known as "New Chinatown." The wide central plaza that still welcomes visitors to Chinatown today was dedicated in a grand gala opening on June 25, 1938.

Located at 947 North Broadway, the plaza features a traditional Chinese gate, an ornate five-tiered pagoda, and a statue of Sun Yat Sen, founder of the Republic of China. Here and throughout Chinatown are dozens of restaurants popular with downtown office workers who can easily walk here, and with theater- and concert-goers headed for the Music Center. Chinatown also offers a tempting array of bakeries, curio shops, and fine-jewelry stores specializing in gold and jade items.

The East Gate of the Old Chinatown Plaza.

Saint Sophia Greek Orthodox Cathedral

It's often said that St. Sophia is the result of a true-life Hollywood story. According to that story, a penniless Greek immigrant, Charles Skouras, vowed he would build a magnificent Orthodox cathedral in Los Angeles if he "made it" in the movie business. Skouras did "make it": He became president of the Twentieth Century–Fox movie studio and was the richest man in America in the 1940s. But the truth is that the idea for a cathedral began with Charles' wife, Florence, a Mormon. Having watched her husband give large sums to a host of beneficiaries over the years—including to the Mormon Church—Florence said that it was high time he did something for "his own people."

After a visit to ancient Hellenic sites, Skouras decided to build an Orthodox cathedral along the lines of the early Greek church in Turkey known as the Hagia Sophia. Completed in 1952 at a cost of $2 million—mostly funded by

Skouras—the plain, massive exterior gives no hint of the rich interior, with its huge chandeliers of imported Czechoslovakian crystal, towering stained-glass windows, and masterfully rendered icons (religious paintings). A large painting of Christ is at the center of the 90-foot-high dome, and another featuring the Virgin and Child is above the exquisite marble altar (normally hidden behind intricate screens).

Because Greeks have always been dispersed throughout the city and county, St. Sophia was never intended as a neighborhood church, but rather as a special place for Orthodox Greeks to gather and worship, particularly on the holiest days of the calendar. In recent years, the surrounding area has been largely populated by Central Americans. Under the guidance of Father John Bakas, the Greeks of St. Sophia have reached out to their neighbors of other faiths, jointly declaring the area a "Byzantine-Latino Quarter."

Korean Bell of Friendship

Located high on a slope above the southern tip of the Palos Verdes Peninsula, the Korean Bell of Friendship is situated so that it looks both east toward the U.S. mainland and west toward the far-off Korean Peninsula. The Republic of Korea presented the bell to the people of Los Angeles in 1976 to mark America's Bicentennial. It was hoped that the traditional symbol of liberty would greet newcomers from Asia in the same way that the Statue of Liberty previously greeted immigrants coming from Europe.

Cast in Korea mainly of copper and tin, the 17-ton bell rests in a traditional pagoda-style pavilion in Angel's Gate Park. The bell is engraved on four sides, each with the same representation of the Goddess of Liberty, but with a different symbol: a yin-yang; a branch of the Rose of Sharon, Korea's national flower; a laurel branch, signifying victory; and a dove of peace. The bell is rung four times each year: on July 4, August 15 (Korean Independence Day), New Year's Eve, and a September day that coincides with Korean Constitution week.

Los Angeles has the largest Korean population outside of Seoul; more than 186,000 were counted in L.A. County in the 2000 census. The city also has a large and lively Koreatown business and nightclub community centered around Wilshire Boulevard and Western Avenue. This concentration is not totally representative of the Korean American community, however, as Koreans have always been well dispersed throughout the metropolitan area; only about 47,000 Korean Americans (about 20 percent of their total population in L.A.) actually live in Koreatown. Those interested in learning more about Korean history and culture should visit the Korean Cultural Center at 5505 Wilshire Boulevard. Avid shoppers may enjoy a visit to the Koreatown Galleria at Olympic Boulevard and Western Avenue.

California African American Museum

People of African American descent have been an important part of Los Angeles' racial and cultural mix from the time the pueblo was founded in 1781. In fact, 26 of the city's original 44 settlers had African ancestors. The first grantee of San Fernando Valley land, Francisco Reyes, was of African descent, as was Pio Pico, the last Mexican governor of California. From the turn of the century until the 1950s, L.A.'s Central Avenue was the heart of a thriving African American community, famed nationwide as a center of black music and culture. Tom Bradley, a descendant of slaves, began a twenty-year run as the city's mayor in 1973.

Despite these contributions, it wasn't until 1984, during the Summer Olympic Games in Los Angeles, that the state museum dedicated to black Americans opened in Exposition Park. Located next to the California Science Center, the museum's mission is to be the "keeper of the flame" of African American history, art, and culture. Recently, it has reworked its somewhat scattered approach to focus on a permanent exhibit titled "The African American Journey West," which encompasses the history and culture of West Africa, the beginnings of the slave trade, the Southern experience, the migration west, and the ongoing contributions of African Americans to the nation.

Newly refurbished (and with plans for further expansion), the 44,000-square-foot museum now contains three full-size galleries, a theater, a conference center, and a spacious sculpture court that accommodates special events. The permanent collection includes more than 3,500 items, and more than 20,000 books, periodicals, and other materials in the museum's research center are available to the public. The museum also hosts a wide range of changing exhibits that focus on entertaining as well as informative aspects of African American life.

Wat Thai

As the most diverse city in the United States, it's no surprise that Los Angeles is home to the largest number of Thais outside of Thailand. Thais began coming to L.A. in significant numbers in the 1970s after immigration restrictions were relaxed for Asians. Of the 80,000 or more now in the city, many live in East Hollywood, a neighborhood that proudly claims two ethnic community signs: "Thai Town" and "Little Armenia."

Miles away, in the heart of the San Fernando Valley, about 40,000 Thais live near Wat Thai, the largest Thai Theravada Buddhist temple in the United States. Built in 1972 near the corner of Roscoe Boulevard and Coldwater Canyon Avenue, the temple is as much a community gathering place as it is a religious site. Although the front door is guarded by two giant warriors, the monks at Wat Thai welcome visitors and are always happy to explain wall hangings and other objects to non-Buddhists. The temple is also highly regarded by L.A. "foodies," who come on weekends to enjoy the many tasty dishes served from booths set up in the temple's courtyard.

Museum of Latin American Art

Considering that Los Angeles was once part of Spain and then Mexico, and that about half the region's residents are of Latin American descent, it's fitting that Los Angeles County is home to the Latin American Museum of Art, the only museum in the country dedicated exclusively to the contemporary arts of Mexico, Central and South America, and the Spanish-speaking islands of the Caribbean. The museum was made possible by the generosity of Robert Gumbiner, a local physician, early HMO founder, and collector of Latin American art. Since its 1996 opening on Alamitos Avenue in Long Beach, the museum's permanent collection, titled "Bridge to the Americas," has grown to

more than 800 works. In June 2007, the museum dedicated a brand new wing and bold new façade, both designed by Mexican architect Manuel Rosen. With the new addition, the museum's total space reached 55,000 square feet, including the outdoor sculpture garden.

Young and energetic, MoLAA (pronounced "moe-la"), as it's known by locals, is as much a cultural center as an art museum. The museum's mission is to educate the public about the unique arts of each Latin American country. Toward that end, the aim of all the museum's many programs, such as "Murals Under the Stars" and "Havana Nights," is to provide cultural context for the works exhibited in the galleries.

Opposite: Francicso Zuniga, "Desnudo Reclinado" ("Reclining Nude"), 1970. Courtesy of Jack Rutberg Fine Arts, Los Angeles.

Index